Cambridge Elements ≡

Elements in American Politics
edited by
Frances E. Lee
Princeton University

T0372741

THE PARTISAN NEXT DOOR

*Stereotypes of Party Supporters
and Consequences for Polarization
in America*

Ethan C. Busby
Brigham Young University

Adam J. Howat
Oberlin College

Jacob E. Rothschild
Reality Check Insights

Richard M. Shafranek
HIT Strategies

CAMBRIDGE
UNIVERSITY PRESS

CAMBRIDGE
UNIVERSITY PRESS

University Printing House, Cambridge CB2 8BS, United Kingdom

One Liberty Plaza, 20th Floor, New York, NY 10006, USA

477 Williamstown Road, Port Melbourne, VIC 3207, Australia

314–321, 3rd Floor, Plot 3, Splendor Forum, Jasola District Centre,
New Delhi – 110025, India

103 Penang Road, #05–06/07, Visioncrest Commercial, Singapore 238467

Cambridge University Press is part of the University of Cambridge.

It furthers the University's mission by disseminating knowledge in the pursuit of
education, learning, and research at the highest international levels of excellence.

www.cambridge.org
Information on this title: www.cambridge.org/9781009100311
DOI: 10.1017/9781009086462

© Ethan C. Busby, Adam J. Howat, Jacob E. Rothschild,
and Richard M. Shafranek 2021

First published 2021

A catalogue record for this publication is available from the British Library.

ISBN 978-1-009-10031-1 Hardback
ISBN 978-1-009-07863-4 Paperback
ISSN 2515-1606 (online)
ISSN 2515-1592 (print)

Additional resources for this publication at www.cambridge.org/busby

The Partisan Next Door

Stereotypes of Party Supporters and Consequences for Polarization in America

Elements in American Politics

DOI: 10.1017/9781009086462
First published online: September 2021

Ethan C. Busby
Brigham Young University

Adam J. Howat
Oberlin College

Jacob E. Rothschild
Reality Check Insights

Richard M. Shafranek
HIT Strategies

Author for correspondence: Adam J. Howat, ahowat@oberlin.edu

Abstract: In the United States, politics has become *tribal* and *personalized*. The influence of partisan divisions has extended beyond the political realm into everyday life, affecting relationships and workplaces as well as the ballot box. To help explain this trend, we examine the stereotypes Americans have of ordinary Democrats and Republicans. Using data from surveys, experiments, and Americans' own words, we explore the content of partisan stereotypes and find that they come in three main flavors – parties as their own tribes, coalitions of other tribes, or vehicles for political issues. These different stereotypes influence partisan conflict; people who hold *trait*-based stereotypes tend to display the highest levels of polarization, while holding *issue*-based stereotypes decreases polarization. This finding suggests that reducing partisan conflict does not require downplaying partisan divisions but shifting the focus to political priorities rather than identity – a turn to what we call responsible partisanship.

Keywords: partisanship, political parties, polarization, stereotypes, social identity

ISBNs: 9781009100311 (HB), 9781009078634 (PB), 9781009086462 (OC)
ISSNs: 2515-1606 (online), 2515-1592 (print)

Contents

A further Online Appendix can be accessed at www.cambridge.org/busby

1 Partisan Conflict and Stereotypes

Partisan conflict in the United States is on the rise. Politicians belonging to the Democratic and Republican Parties have grown further apart in their ideologies and preferences. They have become more entrenched in their positions, less willing to compromise with members of the opposing party to create policy, and less likely to socialize across party lines (e.g., Dietrich, 2021). Increasingly, they even oppose each other over issues on which they agree. Competition over power often takes precedence over policy goals, with lawmakers voting along party lines even when the issues in question – for example, infrastructure, government waste, or ethics oversight – have no clear ideological slant (Lee, 2009). Partisan divisions have scarcely been starker during the modern era.

This conflict has seeped into the attitudes and behavior of ordinary people. A growing number of Americans report seeing major differences between the parties in the United States and say that partisans cannot agree on plans, policies, and basic facts (Pew Research Center, 2019). Partisan conflict has taken on a distinctly personal bent, influencing nonpolitical areas of life. People report a rising dislike for their political adversaries; many describe their opponents as more immoral, unpatriotic, and closed-minded than other Americans (Pew Research Center, 2019). Compared to earlier decades, individuals have grown uncomfortable with romantic relationships between their family members and supporters of political parties they disagree with (Iyengar, Sood, & Lelkes, 2012); the same is true when they make their own romantic decisions (Ballard, 2019). Partisans may discriminate against members of the other party in the workplace (Gift & Gift, 2015), within academia (Inbar & Lammers, 2012), and in everyday economic transactions (Engelhardt & Utych, 2020; McConnell et al., 2018). Rank-and-file partisans seem increasingly unwilling even to live alongside one another.

Examples of this kind of partisan division and conflict abound. One person, for example, took out a roommate ad on Craigslist that warned, "Alcohol, pets, and meat products are not allowed in the house. Neither are Trump supporters" (Rogers, 2017). Similarly, dating sites are becoming tinged with politics, as people list their political views in their romantic profiles. Dating platforms have sprung up to cater to different political groups, including Liberal Hearts (https://liberalhearts.com/), ConservativesOnly (www.conservativesonly.com/), DemocratSingles (www.democratsingles.com/), and Righter (https://wearerigh ter.com/). Those who reach across the social divisions between Democrats and Republicans often face as much scorn as admiration, as demonstrated in a 2019 controversy regarding a public appearance and interpersonal friendship between former president George W. Bush and comedian Ellen DeGeneres. In

Ellen's own words, people wondered, "why is a gay Hollywood liberal sitting next to a conservative Republican president?" (O'Kane, 2019).

These divisions arise from more than just politics. When people learn someone's party identification, they often leap to a number of assumptions about them. These can be as mundane as the clothes partisans wear or the cars they drive, or they might involve stereotypes about deep-seated values – potentially the source of intense, bitter cultural conflict (Brandt & Van Tongeren, 2017; Howat, 2019; Wetherell, Brandt, & Reyna, 2013). Many of these stereotypes become reinforced during election campaigns, when epithets such as "latte liberals" or "gun-toting conservatives" resurface.[1] A well-known attack ad sponsored by the conservative Club for Growth painted 2004 Democratic presidential candidate Howard Dean in explicit detail as a "tax-hiking, government-expanding, latte-drinking, sushi-eating, Volvo-driving, *New York Times*-reading, body-piercing, Hollywood-loving left-wing freak show" (Kelly, 2014).

These phenomena illustrate what social scientists call *polarization* – the widening of divisions between two groups. In the realm of partisan politics, polarization typically refers to ideological divergence between political parties. Ideological polarization in the United States has pushed the Republican and Democratic Parties further and further from one another in their political viewpoints and policy platforms. Political scientists generally agree that this kind of polarization has increased at the elite level in the US over the last several decades (Abramowitz & Saunders, 2008; Fiorina & Abrams, 2008). Such elite-level polarization can strongly influence the political views and attitudes of the public (Druckman, Peterson, & Slothuus, 2013), but it remains a matter of debate whether the ideological distance between the parties' *mass-level supporters* has grown to match their elite counterparts.

Even if such divergence has *not* occurred among the public, mass polarization can result from greater homogeneity within groups. Ordinary citizens have become more ideologically sorted; liberals increasingly identify as Democrats and conservatives as Republicans (Levendusky, 2009). Partisanship has also increasingly aligned with other identities such as race and religion, and this reduction in the number of cross-cutting group divisions further reinforces partisan conflict (Mason, 2018; Mason & Wronski, 2018).

Moreover, the mere *perception* of larger group divisions may contribute to polarization. The American public has, in recent times, made sharper distinctions between the two parties in terms of ideology, policy, and more (Baumer & Gold, 2007; Hetherington, 2001). Even if these impressions do not lead ordinary citizens to polarize, they increase the salience of partisanship as a line of

---

[1] Liberals do, in fact, drink more lattes than conservatives (Mutz & Rao, 2018).

conflict – and, indeed, people have come to see party elites as further apart with respect to policy than they actually are (Levendusky & Malhotra, 2016b). Media portrayals of interparty conflict bolster these misperceptions, often framing partisan debates as conflicts over fundamental values (Levendusky & Malhotra, 2016a; Robison & Mullinix, 2016). In these ways, talk of polarization between Republicans and Democrats can become a self-fulfilling prophecy.

Scholars and pundits alike have lamented these developments, fearing their implications for political compromise and functional governance. The potential repercussions of such polarization extend beyond politics *per se* into the fabric of American social life itself. Supporters of the Democratic and Republican Parties increasingly express a fundamental dislike of their partisan opponents, even in the absence of overt ideological or policy-based disagreements. This phenomenon, which political scientists have labeled *affective polarization*, makes people more likely to register gut-level animosity toward outpartisans, to avoid associating with them even outside political contexts, and to show a willingness to act out against them – even, in rare cases, with violence. In a word, contemporary politics has grown overwhelmingly *tribal*.

What explains this troubling reality? The answer may lie in how individuals think and feel about partisanship itself. A growing body of political science research indicates that party affiliation has become a social identity in its own right, comparable in its nature and consequences to race, religion, or gender (Green, Palmquist, & Schickler, 2002; Greene, 1999, 2004). It not only shapes political orientations and behaviors; it also constitutes, for many individuals, a key component of their self-concepts – and, by extension, how they socially categorize others. This means that partisanship comes with a unique set of *stereotypes* – that is, generalizations about the characteristics of groups and their members (Allport, 1954; Bordalo et al., 2016; Lippmann, 1922). While such mental images help simplify a complex social world, they also may reinforce group-based divisions and engender prejudice (Ahler & Sood, 2018; Eagly & Mladinic, 1989). Extensive study of the nature and consequences of stereotypes provides stark examples of their negative potential. Stereotypes influence whether individuals are selected for positions of prominence and leadership (Galinsky, Hall, & Cuddy, 2013), structure the ways people interpret the behavior of others (Devine, 1989), and interfere with individuals' images of themselves and their performance in a wide range of settings (Steele, 2011; Tine & Gotlieb, 2013). These effects align with the recent expansion of partisan polarization into other social domains, including employment decisions, living arrangements, relationship choices, and more (Gift & Gift, 2015; Iyengar, Sood, & Lelkes, 2012; Mason, 2018; Shafranek, 2020, 2021). The stakes of partisanship and polarization are therefore high and far-reaching.

In the face of such increasingly tribal politics, what, precisely, do the public's mental images of partisans entail? We know that stereotypes predict discrimination, prejudice, and negative actions toward outgroups (as evidenced by research on race, gender, and other social categories). In what ways, then, do ordinary people envision the partisan next door, and how do their ideas intersect with growing concerns about partisan conflict and polarization? And, if partisan stereotypes do contribute to polarization, what can be done about it?

In this Element, we explore these very questions. We seek, first, to document and describe the stereotypes of ordinary partisans held by the public. These mental images can take a variety of forms, including personality traits, memberships in social groups, political issue priorities, and more. Existing work suggests that some people may view their political party as a tribe in itself, with associated characteristics and traits that define them and separate them from the opposing party. We label this view of parties as their own distinctive groups the *partisan-identity* perspective on partisanship. In contrast, some may see the parties as collections of *other* tribes. A variety of groups have aligned themselves to the two major parties in the US for historical, instrumental, and other reasons. Thus, one may think of ordinary supporters primarily as members of other groups (e.g., racial, economic, religious) pursuing group-based interests through their party attachments. We call this the *coalitional* perspective. Finally, other people's stereotypes might emphasize the political issues that animate partisans. Such stereotypes describe partisans as caring about different policies or modes of government (and the parties, by implication, as vehicles for those political preferences). This view appears distinct from the other two, as it lacks explicitly tribal components and, on a deeper level, involves some degree of internalization of the priorities and values of other people, copartisan and outpartisan alike. Borrowing from other researchers (Huddy, Mason, & Aarøe, 2015), we label this the *instrumental* perspective.

Our analyses, using text-based data and machine learning, reveal all three kinds of partisan stereotypes among the public. All of these perspectives on partisanship see partisans as divided in some significant way. We see consistent evidence that people do perceive meaningful differences between rank-and-file Democrats and Republicans, regardless of whether they hold predominantly partisan-identity, coalitional, or instrumental stereotypes. But our analysis of the consequences of these stereotypes suggests that what people see as the *source* of partisan divisions is critical. Those who hold images of party supporters more in line with the partisan-identity perspective demonstrate stronger polarization along both affective and ideological lines. A more instrumental perspective, in contrast, does not show the same patterns.

Many people hold stereotypes of all three kinds. People's mental images of partisans do not seem to be neatly split into these three camps; instead, they hold some partisan-identity, coalitional, and instrumental ideas at the same time. While perhaps unsurprising, this observation has powerful implications. If people hold all three kinds of stereotypes, those interested in reducing partisan conflict may shift *which* stereotypes individuals emphasize – a considerably easier task than creating stereotypes that do not already exist. Decades of research in psychology and political science indicates that shifting the focus of stereotypes can be accomplished with relatively minimal interventions or simple media messages (Devine, 1989; Sassenberg & Moskowitz, 2005). We implement this very idea in a survey experiment and find that prompting people to focus on instrumental stereotypes reduces affective and ideological polarization, especially compared to partisan-identity stereotypes.

Based on all of these findings, we conclude that one solution to polarization is not to ignore or de-emphasize the differences between political parties. Real partisan divides exist, and people often hold overexaggerated versions of these differences in their minds (Ahler & Sood, 2018); as a result, convincing the public that the parties are not divided would likely prove an insurmountable task. We suggest, instead, that focusing on a specific *type* of difference – one that encourages people to think about what partisans value and advocate for in terms of policy – can attenuate the partisan polarization that has come to define the modern era in the United States.

1.1 Overview of the Element

The rest of this Element proceeds as follows. In Section 2, we expand upon the theoretical and empirical foundations of the partisan-identity, instrumental, and coalitional perspectives. We relate these different understandings of partisanship to the concept of stereotypes as described by social psychologists, and to previous research in political science documenting the public's mental images of the parties and their relationship to polarization. Drawing on insights from this work, we lay out our expectations concerning the effects of partisan-identity, coalitional, and instrumental stereotypes of partisans on polarization: partisan-identity images should exacerbate it, whereas instrumental images should decrease polarization.

In Section 3, we provide a descriptive account of the stereotypes ordinary citizens hold about ordinary partisans. We detail two large-scale surveys, conducted in 2016 and 2018, in which we solicit people's open-ended descriptions of rank-and-file party supporters. Using a form of machine-learning text analysis (structural topic modeling, or STM) to identify patterns in these

responses, we find that people's mental images cohere with the three conceptions of partisanship predicted by our theoretical framework. Partisan-identity
stereotypes appear to be the most common, highlighting the prevalence of tribal
thinking around partisanship. We also observe a great deal of consistency in the
responses provided by self-identified Democrats, Republicans, and independents, and we find that respondents tend to associate the correct issues and groups
with the two parties. On partisan-identity stereotypes, there is somewhat more
cross-party disagreement; people concur to a large extent regarding partisans'
typical traits, but they also ascribe positive traits to their inparty and negative
ones to the outparty.

Section 4 explores the political and social consequences of these stereotypes, using observational and experimental data. We find, first, that individuals who express more partisan-identity (rather than instrumental or
coalitional) stereotypes also exhibit greater polarization. They show wider
gaps in their affective evaluations of the parties, they view the parties as
ideologically further apart, and they tend to be more extreme in their
ideological self-placement. To ascertain the causal nature of these relationships, we leverage an experimental treatment in our 2018 survey inducing
respondents to think about ordinary partisans in partisan-identity, instrumental, or coalitional ways. We find that imagining party supporters in
instrumental terms significantly decreases affective and ideological polarization, relative to all other experimental conditions. Meanwhile, subjects in
the partisan-identity and control conditions demonstrate similar levels of
polarization – sensible given that we find partisan-identity-focused stereotypes to be the most common among the public. Taken together, our
analyses show the content of party images to be highly consequential for
polarization.

We conclude in Section 5 with the implications of our findings for polarization and democratic functioning in the United States. Members of the
public appear to hold clear, varied, and cohesive images of mass-level party
supporters. These stereotypes, moreover, prove politically consequential, with
those who view partisanship in tribal terms more polarized. However, those
who imagine partisans largely in terms of the issues they consider important
prove to be less polarized. We discuss what this means for the future of
partisan conflict, offering as a possible solution a mindset we call *responsible
partisanship*, in which partisans seek to understand themselves and their
opponents not as fundamentally different kinds of people, but as groups
with different issue priorities. Such perspective-taking has the potential to
reduce polarization not just in the political domain but in other areas of social
life.

2 Party Images in the American Electorate

Let us begin this section with a thought exercise. Picture in your mind a person who supports the Democratic Party. Try and come up with some specific, concrete details about that individual. What are they like? How would you describe them? Now, do the same thing for a supporter of the Republican Party. What is this person like? If you had to summarize your mental images of each person in only four or five words, what would you say?

What kinds of images came to your mind? Was it hard to come up with something for one or both people? Did you mainly think about the two partisans' personalities or character? Perhaps you focused on their demographic characteristics, or other groups to which they belong. Then again, maybe what came most easily into your head were the political issues those people would consider most important, or maybe something else altogether. Moreover, how did you react to the mental images you conjured? How did you find yourself *feeling* about these hypothetical individuals?

We take up questions like these in this Element. The mental images people have of Republicans and Democrats are not just an interesting thought experiment; they reflect people's attitudes toward politics, their views of themselves, and a deep-rooted sense of attachment to the political parties in the United States. Your answers to the questions above can reveal something important about your own party identification and the role it plays in your life.

Party affiliation constitutes one of the most important and influential phenomena in American politics. Political scientists have recognized this reality for decades, and since the publication of *The American Voter* (Campbell et al., 1960), partisanship has become one of the most heavily studied constructs within the discipline. It may be the most salient division in American politics today, contributing to conflict not merely in government and the voting booth, but also in everyday social life. With supporters of the two major parties increasingly polarized, knowing how rank-and-file partisans envision each other may prove key to understanding political conflict in the US.

What, then, are the images that ordinary people hold of ordinary Democratic and Republican supporters? How would most Americans answer the questions above? Do they picture mass-level partisans in terms of individual personality and character traits, like open-mindedness, patriotism, and prejudice? Do they instead emphasize the political issues partisans care about, such as abortion, healthcare, national security, and taxes? Are these stereotypes based on the other group memberships, such as race, gender, or class? Or do they take an altogether different form?

Existing work on party identification in the United States offers some clues about what these images might contain. Research in political science usually conceptualizes partisanship in three main ways – what we labelled in Section 1 as the *partisan-identity, instrumental*, and *coalitional* views. In this section, we describe these perspectives in more detail, discuss their origins and persistence in existing political science scholarship, and link these disparate versions of partisanship to psychological processes of stereotyping among the mass electorate. Finally, we discuss the potential consequences of these different kinds of stereotypes for polarization.

2.1 Three Conceptions of Partisanship

A growing body of research, particularly in political psychology, conceives of partisanship as a social category in its own right (e.g., Green, Palmquist, & Schickler, 2002; Greene, 1999, 2004; Huddy, Mason, & Aarøe, 2015; Theodoridis, 2017). Partisanship, from this perspective, functions as its own *social identity*, or the part of an individual's self-concept which derives from knowledge of their membership in the group and the emotional significance they attach to that membership (Tajfel, 1981, 255). Green, Palmquist, and Schickler expound that party identification "involves comparing a judgment about oneself with one's perception of a social group. As people reflect on whether they are Democrats or Republicans (or neither), they call to mind some mental image, or stereotype, of what these sorts of people are like and square those images with their own self-conceptions" (2002, 8). Antecedents of this perspective can be seen in the foundational work of Campbell and colleagues (1960), who emphasize that party affiliation is an enduring psychological attachment, not merely the decision to vote for a party's candidates or evaluations of its platforms or performance. We call this perspective the *partisan-identity* view of partisanship because, importantly, it involves conceiving of party affiliation as a social identity in its own right, not merely as connected to other group identities such as race or religion.[2]

Partisan groups in this framework need not be especially programmatic or ideological. What matters, instead, is an individual's subjective sense of attachment to the party and commonality with other party supporters – and, by extension, a feeling of dissimilarity from supporters of the opposing party. A strong partisan social identity can lead to anger in the face of political loss (Huddy, Mason, & Aarøe, 2015), dehumanization of political opponents

---

[2] Previous work (e.g., Abramowitz & Saunders, 2006) has used the term "identity" to refer to partisanship's connections to other social identities. For the sake of a clear distinction from partisan-identity specifically, we instead use the terms "coalitional" and "groups," as noted below, to describe this perspective.

(Cassese, 2019; Martherus et al., 2021), judgments about partisans' moral character (Clifford, 2020; Goggin & Theodoridis, 2017; Hayes, 2005), and the ascription of positive traits to the inparty and negative traits to the outparty (Iyengar, Sood, & Lelkes, 2012; Iyengar & Westwood, 2015; Iyengar et al., 2019). The partisan-identity view of partisanship is thus likely to exacerbate partisan conflict and polarization.

This perspective diverges from a more traditional view of partisanship that emphasizes issue positions or general ideological orientations. According to this traditional perspective, individuals consider their preexisting policy preferences and/or their generally liberal or conservative orientation, and these things in turn drive them to affiliate with one party or the other. This view goes back to some of political science's most foundational works (e.g., Key, 1964), as well as finding support in more recent research (e.g., Abramowitz & Saunders, 2006; Fiorina, Abrams, & Pope, 2005; Niemi & Jennings, 1991). Through this lens, people view their party and the outparty less as cohesive social groups and more as a means to pursue various interests and policy goals. Following Huddy, Mason, and Aarøe (2015), we call this the *instrumental* view of partisanship.

Occupying a conceptual space between the partisan-identity and instrumental perspectives is partisanship based on other social group memberships. Such groups may include race, gender, class, religious affiliation, and more. Under this perspective, which also dates back to classic scholarship (Berelson, Lazarsfeld, & McPhee, 1954; Converse, 1964), parties act as vehicles for the political interests of the groups to which supporters belong. Recent work continues to affirm the importance of group memberships to party affiliation (Achen & Bartels, 2016; Kinder & Kalmoe, 2017; Ahler & Sood, 2018; Robison & Moskowitz, 2019) and, for many citizens, the party itself may take a back seat to these other groups. For example, race has long been a driver of partisanship in the United States, and work consistently finds that the racial composition of the parties shapes party attachments (Key, 1949; Carmines & Stimson, 1989; Hutchings & Valentino, 2004; Abrajano & Hajnal, 2017; Kuziemko & Washington, 2018). Partisanship, from this view, is a combination of attitudes toward the *other* social groups that attach themselves to political parties and the goals those groups pursue. We term this the *coalitional* view of partisanship, and it resembles the instrumental perspective in that the parties predominantly serve a set of narrower interests.[3] However, it also

---

[3] In previous work (Rothschild et al., 2019), we find that issue- and group-based stereotypes tend to occur together. Our read of past research and our own theorizing at the time prompted us to combine both types of party images under the instrumental label. However, refinement of our theory and the collection of new empirics has led us to treat the instrumental and coalitional perspectives as distinct.

overlaps with the partisan-identity perspective; both involve attachments to social groups. As Green, Palmquist, and Schickler (2002) explain, social group memberships rank among the most important aspects of partisans' self-concepts when they consider whether to side with Democrats or Republicans. Moreover, Converse (1964) classically observed group interests to be the most common drivers of people's political beliefs.

None of these views are wholly incompatible with each other. Some major works on partisanship, in fact, provide strong evidence for more than one of them (e.g., Campbell et al., 1960; Green, Palmquist, & Schickler, 2002; Sniderman & Stiglitz, 2012). The sorting of various social groups into clear partisan camps can promote the coalitional version of partisanship, but may also heighten partisanship's influence as an independent social identity (Mason & Wronski, 2018; Mason, 2018). Issue-based elements of partisanship may also overlap and combine with the two other alternatives discussed above. Individual voters may employ multiple perspectives simultaneously, or different individuals may be prone to seeing partisanship in one way or another.

These are the questions we aim to answer in this Element: How prevalent are these different perspectives in the public consciousness? Do people tend to see ordinary partisans in partisan-identity, instrumental, or coalitional terms? Are the distinctions between these versions of partisanship as clear for the public as they are among academics? What differences exist between those who tend to think of partisanship in these disparate ways? Finally, what are the consequences of holding these different views for partisan conflict? One place to look for these answers is in the stereotypes that people hold of partisans.

2.2 Stereotyping Partisans

Bordalo et al. (2016, 1755) describe stereotypes as "intuitive generalizations that individuals routinely use in their everyday life" to help make sense of the complex social world while not overtaxing one's cognitive resources. Stereotypes arise from real or perceived group differences and usually involve comparing one group to another (Bordalo et al., 2016; Sherman et al., 2009). Socialization (Bigler & Liben, 2007), the media (Rahn & Cramer, 1996), direct experiences with different social groups (Sherman, 1996), and different internal characteristics and motivations (Mackie et al., 1996) all influence the development of stereotypes. Stereotypes are not necessarily positive or negative, and people use them frequently in social and political life.

Extensive research in psychology indicates that (1) people develop stereotypes of most (if not all) of the groups they encounter, (2) these stereotypes can focus on different elements (such as traits, behaviors, or beliefs), and (3) these generalizations have a profound impact on individuals' behavior and attitudes. For example, the stereotype that African Americans do not uphold values of hard work and self-reliance has been linked to opposing policies such as affirmative action and workplace diversity initiatives (Brandt & Reyna, 2012). Expectations about women's greater "niceness" or communality can lead to backlash and discrimination against women who behave in more assertive ways (Rudman & Glick, 2001). We have ample reason to believe that stereotypes in the realm of partisanship should be just as consequential.

Political scientists have incorporated these ideas in the study of political behavior, parties, and public opinion. One of the earliest discussions of stereo-types was explicitly concerned with public opinion and the functioning of democracies; Lippmann (1922) wrote extensively about the images in the minds of the public and how those representations were distorted and limited generalizations of the real world. According to Lippmann, relying on these kinds of stereotypes had important democratic consequences and left the public open to manipulation by those with power and resources. While subsequent researchers did not necessarily share Lippmann's pessimism, political scientists have built on these ideas. Some studies focus on how stereotypes of political parties serve as useful guides for citizens when evaluating candidates (Rahn, 1993; Rahn & Cramer, 1996), forming stances on political issues (Brewer, 2009; Geer, 1991; Pope & Woon, 2009), and selecting which party to identify with in the first place (Green, Palmquist, & Schickler, 2002).

This work is part of a larger body of research on Americans' images of the parties. Most has focused on the parties as a whole – images of "the Democratic Party" or "the Republican Party." Some early work observed that "the images that the parties project . . . and the ways in which the voters perceive the parties seem to be the major determinants of political alignment" (Sellers, 1965, 27; see also Matthews & Prothro, 1966). From this perspective, the images political parties promote to the public help explain the rise and fall of each party's fortunes across election cycles; implicitly, this view treats the parties primarily as collections of politicians or as organizations, giving less attention to their rank-and-file supporters. Recent work by Druckman and Levendusky (2019) finds that, indeed, when prompted to think of the opposing party in general terms, most people tend to think of party elites rather than the party's mass membership. Nonetheless, even this early discussion attributed great import-ance to the numbers of mass-level "identifiers" and their motivations to identify with one party or the other.

Other scholars have attempted to map the images of the parties that reside in Americans' minds. A key set of questions from the American National Election Studies (ANES) have, for many years, solicited individuals' views of the

Democratic and Republican Parties. These items ask respondents to describe, in an open-ended fashion, what they like and/or dislike about each party. A few scholars have dug deeply into these questions, looking to categorize and group responses into meaningful images of the parties. One approach grouped these likes and dislikes into a few broad categories: the people in the party, the party as manager of government, the party's broad philosophy, or its domestic or foreign policy positions (Trilling, 1976). Others have developed more complex categorizations; an analysis of ANES data from 1960 to 1984 suggested grouping responses into general philosophy, economic, social issue, foreign policy, government management, and other responses (Sanders, 1988). An even larger endeavor, focusing on data from these questions from 1952 to 2004, observes similar categories of responses: economic, non-economic domestic, foreign policy, party philosophy, general management, general party image, and people in the party (Brewer, 2009). In these latter two cases, issue-based themes seem especially important and relate in important ways to party identification.

These findings, along with a focus on issue-centric stereotypes of the parties at an elite level, have dominated much of the research on party images or stereotypes. A paradigmatic example advances a theory of "issue ownership," in which voters systematically view one party or the other as better able to handle different issues and issue domains (Petrocik, 1996). Democrats tend to be seen as more capable when it comes to social welfare issues (e.g., education, healthcare), whereas Republicans more often have an advantage in foreign policy, defense, and social order (e.g., crime). A candidate from a given party may emphasize the issues their party "owns," influencing the criteria by which voters make their decisions – a strategy that presidential candidates have successfully employed for the better part of the last century (Petrocik, Benoit, & Hansen, 2003; Pope & Woon, 2009). In the absence of more specific information, people by and large attribute party-stereotypical issue positions to candidates (Conover & Feldman, 1989). Further, individuals typically infer a host of stereotypical issue stances even when the candidates' own statements exhibit inconsistencies with the party line (Rahn, 1993).[4] The accessibility of this kind of partisan stereotype can be influenced by the media environment, especially among the more politically sophisticated (Rahn & Cramer, 1996). The behavioral and attitudinal consequences of these stereotypes, therefore, can depend on accessibility and relevance.

Stereotypes of parties have gone beyond issue-based reputations. The theory of "trait ownership" builds directly on issue ownership, connecting the issues

---

[4] However, depending on the applicability of individuating information to the judgments at hand, issue positions may play a greater role (Crawford et al., 2011).

owned by the parties to associated personal traits. Republican presidential candidates are seen as stronger leaders and more moral, owing to their emphasis on individualism, law and order, family values, and defense. Meanwhile, people view Democratic candidates, given their focus on social welfare issues and helping vulnerable groups, as more compassionate or empathetic. Like issue ownership, trait ownership may become reinforced by episodic political conflict and the media environment, with powerful effects on vote choice (Hayes, 2005). In addition to these trait-focused images, Americans have come to view the parties in gendered terms (Winter, 2010). Analysis of the ANES like-dislike responses, supplemented with experimental data, indicates that Republicans are seen as more "masculine" (active, independent, and decisive) and Democrats as more "feminine" (compassionate, other-focused, emotional, and kind). Cognitive links between the parties and these traditionally gendered terms operate not just at the conscious, explicit level, but at a deeper, implicit level as well. It appears that the electorate thinks of the parties not just in terms of salient issues, but also in terms of highly personal trait expectancies.

The research discussed above has significantly advanced our understanding of party images. Americans have stereotypes of the parties, typically focused on party elites, with partisan-identity, coalitional, and instrumental components. However, it leaves two major lacunae to be explored, one substantive and one more methodological. In terms of substance, past work has focused almost exclusively on the parties as a whole or on party elites (e.g., candidates) – which may be one and the same in the minds of most voters (Druckman & Levendusky, 2019). Stereotypes of party elites are undoubtedly important to politics; after all, these are the people primarily being evaluated by citizens when they cast their ballots.

However, partisan conflict does not occur only in the context of elections or policymaking. Partisanship has become a *social* and not merely political identity (Green, Palmquist, & Schickler, 2002; Greene, 1999, 2004), with implications for its role in Americans' lives. Partisanship can color employment decisions (Gift & Gift, 2015), relationship choices (Iyenger, Sood, & Lelkes, 2012; Huber & Malhotra, 2017), and roommate preferences (Shafranek, 2021). To understand the partisan polarization of the current era, which commonly extends beyond the political arena into other domains of social life (Iyengar et al., 2019; Mason, 2018; Shafranek, 2020), we must examine the content and consequences of *mass-level* partisan stereotypes. Intergroup conflict is profoundly influenced by individuals' stereotypes of the people around them, and these mental images can have cascading cognitive, emotional, and social consequences (Allport, 1954; Chen & Bargh, 1997; Berinsky & Mendelberg, 2005). To better understand partisan conflict, then, we ask: What do people think of the partisans living next door? How do stereotypes of ordinary party supporters shape political attitudes and behavior?

In a more methodological vein, existing studies of partisan stereotypes display a common set of limitations. Many (e.g., Iyengar, Sood, & Lelkes, 2012; Winter, 2010) use closed-ended items to measure stereotypes, effectively taking for granted the range of salient images people may hold. While these kinds of measures provide important insight into how much people endorse specific stereotypes, they can only speak to the specific ideas included in such questions. To avoid this issue, parallel studies in psychology often start with several rounds of open-ended responses to distill a closed-item list of the key components of individuals' stereotypes of groups (e.g., Madon et al., 2001). To our knowledge, however, such sequential work has never been done in political science. The research that employs closed-ended items about partisan stereotypes either draws on frequently used items within this literature or researchers' intuitions about what terms to use. Those that do utilize open-ended responses (e.g., Brewer, 2009; Sanders, 1988; Trilling, 1976) often lump participants' answers into a relatively small number of (sometimes preconceived) categories or rely on a set of pre-coded categories from the ANES. While, again, this work has yielded valuable insights, its findings may mask some important nuances – not only in terms of what ideas come to mind when people think about partisans, but also how different stereotypes relate to each other and the broader themes they reflect.

The research presented in this Element helps to fill both of these gaps. We solicit Americans' ideas about ordinary people who support the Democratic and Republican Parties, seeking to understand how partisans think of themselves and each other. Moreover, we employ new methods of analysis to bring as few *a priori* assumptions as possible to our examination of partisan stereotype content. We follow the procedures used by other psychologists, employing open-ended questions, analyzing those data, and then developing closed-item measures in later data collections. Section 3 describes this process in detail. Finally, we provide the most encompassing investigation to date of the political and social *consequences* of these stereotypes.

2.3 Partisan Stereotypes and Polarization

Despite their utility in simplifying and navigating the social world, stereotypes are not without costs. Assumptions and generalizations about different groups have the potential to exacerbate intergroup conflict and increase prejudice (Allport, 1954; Ahler & Sood, 2018). Expectations of groups and group members influence the behavior of the groups doing the stereotyping as well as those being stereotyped, with negative psychological and even physiological consequences (Steele, 2011). Implicit components of stereotypes can lead to social inequalities and also increase resistance to changing incorrect images of social groups (Bodenhausen & Wyer, 1985; Reuben, Sapienza, & Zingales, 2014). Because the inaccurate and accurate components are cognitively linked, even explicitly rejected negative stereotypes can shape interpersonal and political evaluations (Berinsky & Mendelberg, 2005).

In the case of partisanship specifically, stereotypes – of one's own party and of the outparty – may exert considerable influence over the intense polarization that characterizes the modern era (Abramowitz & Saunders, 2008; Baumer & Gold, 2007; Iyengar et al., 2019; Mason, 2018). Recent work finds that partisans at the mass level have, at the least, become more polarized in *affective* terms. That is, partisans have increasingly come to dislike supporters of the opposing party on a deep, emotional level, and they express a greater desire for social distance from such individuals (Iyengar et al., 2019; c.f., Klar, Krupnikov, & Ryan, 2018). For example, Iyengar, Sood, and Lelkes (2012, 417) find that, in 2010, nearly 50 percent of Republicans and over 30 percent of Democrats reported that they would be unhappy if their offspring were to marry a member of the opposing party – an increase by roughly a factor of five compared to respondents in 1960. This phenomenon results at least in part from partisanship's growing importance as a social identity (Iyengar et al., 2019; Mason, 2018), but it remains to be seen how affective polarization relates to specific mental images of rank-and-file partisans.

Though the degree of *ideological* polarization among ordinary voters remains a matter of debate (e.g., Abramowitz & Saunders, 2008; Fiorina & Abrams, 2008), political scientists broadly agree that such polarization has grown at the elite level. This rise has, in turn, increased the salience of partisanship among the public, with Americans apt to perceive meaningful differences between Democrats and Republicans (Baumer & Gold, 1995, 2007; Hetherington, 2001; Levendusky, 2010). The current political climate, then, seems ripe for the development of a wide range of stereotypes about partisans and their characteristics, and because stereotypes tend to reflect the broader social and political environment (Bordalo et al., 2016; Josefson, 2000; Rahn & Cramer, 1996), citizens' images of party supporters likely both respond and contribute to polarization.

We expect partisan stereotypes to relate to both ideological and affective forms of polarization. While different literatures explore these two forms of polarization, in individuals' minds, they may be mutually reinforcing (Rogowski & Sutherland 2016; Webster & Abramowitz, 2017; Banda & Cluverius, 2018). Research on party stereotypes also provides reasons to expect both kinds of polarization to be linked to mental representations of partisans. For example, party images related to political issues magnify perceptions of issue-based disagreement between the two parties (Bordalo et al., 2016; Chambers et al., 2006). Furthermore, simply holding a greater *number* of distinct stereotypes about the parties, regardless of their specific content, has been associated with having more extreme ideological views (Baumer & Gold, 2007). Past work has also shown that, with the rise of affective polarization, partisans have become more likely to ascribe positive traits to their own party and negative traits to the outparty (Iyengar, Sood, & Lelkes, 2012). This comports with social identity theory, which posits that, in order to maintain a positive self-concept, individuals tend toward more positive evaluations of the groups to which they belong and strive to accentuate that ingroup's differences from outgroups (Hogg & Abrams, 1988; Tajfel & Turner, 1979).

Figure 1 illustrates our theoretical expectations linking different kinds of partisan stereotypes to polarization, as well as the potential psychological mechanisms behind different stereotypes' effects. Because instrumental stereotypes focus on issue priorities, they highlight purely political differences between partisans, rather than identity-based divisions. Further, the mental task of reporting instrumental stereotypes of partisans requires a mild amount of perspective-taking, thinking through what partisans believe and why. This type of mental exercise has been shown to reduce group-based prejudice and provide a route out of conflict and polarization (e.g., Todd et al., 2011; Simonovits, Kézdi, & Kardos, 2018). These processes are described in the leftmost path of Figure 1. Because instrumental stereotypes involve stepping back from one's own partisan identity and into other partisans' shoes, we expect their use to reduce partisan conflict and polarization.[5]

Coalitional stereotypes should have a mixed relationship with polarization, illustrated by the center line of Figure 1. On one hand, they may prime various non-partisan identities (such as race and gender) that could then go on to exacerbate partisan conflict. On the other, coalitional stereotypes are also likely to emphasize cross-pressures – making salient that people belong to some, but not all, of the groups connected to the parties – with the potential to reduce polarization and extremity (Berelson, Lazarsfeld, & McPhee, 1954; Brader, Tucker, & Therriault, 2014). They also may engage social norms about specific social groups (e.g., racial egalitarianism, anti-sexism) that depress the polarizing potential of these kinds of stereotypes; discrimination against nonpolitical groups remains much less acceptable in the minds of most Americans (Iyengar

---

[5] Some recent work, however, does link policy-based disagreement to affective polarization (Orr & Huber, 2021).

& Westwood, 2015). Coalitional stereotypes, then, likely occupy a middle space between the instrumental and partisan-identity views.

Drawing on social identity theory, we contend that thinking of partisanship in more partisan-identity terms should predict greater polarization (see the right-hand path of Figure 1). The more people conceive of typical partisans in terms of individual-level traits – consistent with thinking of one's political party as a social group in itself – the more likely they are to think in essentialist terms (see Levy, Stroessner, & Dweck, 1998). From this perspective, partisans are divided not only by different beliefs, priorities, or group memberships; they represent fundamentally different kinds of people. This *personalization* of partisanship promotes sharper group-based thinking about Republicans and Democrats, encouraging a stronger emphasis on the inparty/outparty distinction. Success for one party necessarily means loss for the other, and holding moderate attitudes toward opponents may be seen as disloyalty or betrayal. All of these processes should lead to greater partisan polarization and conflict. The

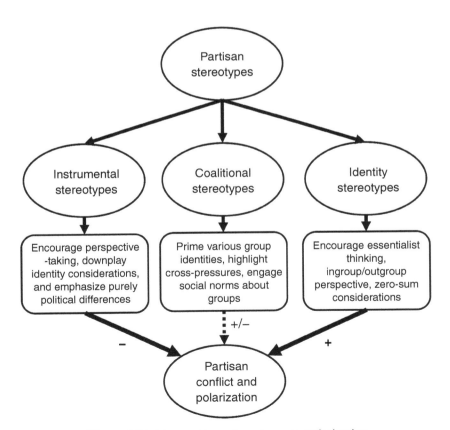

Figure 1 Linking partisan stereotypes to polarization

more individuals personalize partisanship, the more emotional and ideological distance they will feel and perceive between ordinary Republicans and Democrats.

In the next two sections, we tackle these questions and expectations in two ways. First, we document the content of partisan stereotypes in the United States, how much agreement exists among the public around these mental images, and how they correspond with the partisan-identity, coalitional, and instrumental versions of partisanship. Second, we evaluate the consequences of identity-based, coalitional, and instrumental partisan stereotypes on affective and ideological polarization. We find evidence that the public subscribes to the different views of partisanship discussed above. Moreover, what people think of when conjuring up a typical Democrat or Republican matters, in ways that are both academically illuminating and socially important to ordinary Americans.

3 The Content of Partisan Stereotypes

Many differences exist between Republicans and Democrats, some political and some not. Republicans are far more concerned about the economy and taxes than Democrats; Democrats put more emphasis on climate change and income inequality than Republicans (Newport, 2018). Librarians, pediatricians, and bartenders are overwhelmingly Democrats; petroleum geologists, farmers, and car salesmen are disproportionately Republicans (Swanson, 2015; Verdant Labs, 2015). Republicans have names like Wayne, Dale, and Randy; Dylans, Ethans, and Isaiahs are more likely to be found among Democrats (Nelson, 2014). Democrats buy more chicken tikka masala, lentil soup, and BLTs; Republicans prefer sweet-and-sour chicken, wonton soup, and buffalo chicken wraps (Wilson, 2016).

Are Americans aware of these differences? Which have percolated into their stereotypes of Republicans and Democrats? Are certain kinds of stereotypes more common than others? Have people's images of partisans lined up with partisan-identity, instrumental, or coalitional considerations? Or do they fall along other lines?

To answer these questions and empirically evaluate the ideas proposed in Section 2, we conducted two large-scale surveys in 2016 and 2018. We asked Americans open-ended questions to document their mental images of party supporters – the Democrats and Republicans they encounter in everyday life. The task we use to document these images matches closely the thought exercise presented in Section 2. This enables us to learn what ideas come to mind when people imagine rank-and-file partisans, unfiltered by our own presumptions about what that stereotype content should look like.

Using both sets of survey data, we describe individuals' views of ordinary partisans and how they relate to the partisan-identity, instrumental, and coalitional perspectives. We use structural topic modeling (STM; see Roberts et al., 2014), a form of machine-learning text analysis, to identify the patterns in individuals' open-ended descriptions of partisans in the 2016 data. These ideas cohere around distinct themes – traits, issue positions, and group memberships – which we link to the three conceptions of partisanship described in Section 2. We also use these results to help generate items presented in the 2018 survey, which ask respondents to indicate the traits, groups, or issues from predetermined lists that fit typical Democrats and Republicans.

We reach four main conclusions. First, we find evidence of all three types of partisanship; people use partisan-identity, instrumental, and coalitional language to talk about typical party supporters. Second, there is considerable overlap between the views Democrats, Republicans, and independents express of partisans, suggesting widespread, shared stereotypes among the American public. Third, many people correctly associate political issues and groups with the corresponding parties. We also find substantial agreement across parties concerning supporters' typical traits, though respondents tend to ascribe positive traits to their copartisans and negative ones to outpartisans. Fourth, a substantial proportion of respondents default to trait-based stereotypes of party supporters, giving credence to the notion that partisanship functions increasingly as a social identity of its own (Green, Palmquist, & Schickler, 2002; Greene, 1999, 2004; Mason, 2018). In the rest of this section, we discuss our research goals, the details of our two empirical studies, and the results from both surveys.

3.1 Goals

The primary objective of this section is to document the stereotypes of ordinary partisans. While the literatures from political science and psychology give us some general expectations – that, for example, individuals are likely to possess substantive stereotypes of partisans and that partisan-identity, instrumental, and coalitional views should all be present – these are not testable hypotheses in the traditional sense. We focus instead on documenting and describing stereotypes, therefore, rather than conducting statistical tests or supporting a specific hypothesis.

Given the lack of existing research in this area, this constitutes a crucial first step to understanding the images people have of partisans and the ways those images connect to partisan polarization. Such descriptive research has value on its own terms (Gerring, 2012; Kreuzer, 2019) and is common in studies of stereotypes generally (Katz & Braly, 1933; Gilbert, 1951; Eagly & Mladinic,

1989; Devine & Elliot, 1995). Descriptive studies of this kind are also essential for causally oriented science, as "it is hard to develop [causal] explanations before we know something about the world and what needs to be explained" (King, Keohane, & Verba, 1994, 34). This section provides important insight into the minds of American citizens and serves as a foundation for the causal inferences we present in Section 4.

We turn now to the two original surveys we conducted in 2016 and 2018. In both, we use open-ended questions asking people to list the ideas that came to mind about supporters of the Republican and Democratic Parties. In the 2018 data, we add a set of closed-ended items based on the open-ended responses found in the 2016 data. We begin by discussing the 2016 data and then discuss the additional contributions from the 2018 survey.

3.2 2016 Design and Methods

Our first survey occurred around the 2016 presidential primaries. We administered a version of it to three different samples: undergraduates at a large private Midwestern university (N = 548), participants in an online labor market (Amazon's Mechanical Turk or MTurk; N = 954), and a nationally diverse non-probability sample collected through Research Now[6] (N = 861). The undergraduate sample was collected between March and April 2016, the MTurk sample in April 2016, and the national sample in early August 2016. Table 1 provides demographic information about these different samples. The inclusion of multiple kinds of samples jibes with prior work on stereotype content, which makes frequent use of student samples (Katz & Braly, 1933; Devine & Elliot, 1995; Madon et al., 2001), MTurk samples (Scherer, Windschitl, & Graham, 2015), and other convenience samples (Graham, Nosek, & Haidt, 2012). Existing research also demonstrates the utility of drawing inferences from various kinds of convenience samples (Druckman & Kam, 2011; Mullinix et al., 2015; Levay, Freese, & Druckman, 2016). Further, our analyses explicitly incorporate differences between samples, as discussed in detail below.

The survey proceeded in the same way for each sample. Borrowing a technique from social psychology (Eagly & Mladinic, 1989), we first asked respondents to list their stereotypes of rank-and-file partisans ("words that typically describe people who support the [Democratic/Republican] Party"); they were prompted to provide four words or phrases for each party separately. We asked first about general descriptions of partisans, and then asked subjects to complete parallel items specifically about the personality traits, groups, and issues they associated with supporters

---

[6] This research firm has since been renamed Dynata (www.dynata.com/press/announcing-new-name-and-brand-research-now-ssi-is-now-dynata/).

Table 1 Sample demographic characteristics (2016 data)

	Percent of Sample		
	Undergraduate	*MTurk*	*National*
Female	52	60	52
Democrat	75	55	45
Independent[7]	6	16	18
Republican	19	29	37
Liberal	67	49	32
Moderate	17	24	31
Conservative	15	27	37
Nonwhite	37	15	20
		Sample median	
Family Income ($)	150,000 to 200,000	50,000 to 75,000	50,000 to 75,000
Education	All have some college	Two-year college degree	Bachelor's degree
Political Interest	5 out of 7	5 out of 7	5 out of 7

Source: Reprinted by permission from Springer Nature: Springer, *Political Behavior*, "Pigeonholing Partisans: Stereotypes of Party Supporters and Partisan Polarization," Jacob E. Rothschild et al., 2018.

of the parties. These specific areas correspond directly to the three views of partisanship explained in Section 2. This kind of question provides a direct view into respondents' thoughts (Iyengar, 1996; Roberts et al., 2014) and avoids making assumptions about what these stereotypes include (Devine, 1989; Eagly & Mladinic, 1989). Open-ended responses have a long history in political science (e.g., Converse, 1964), and are increasingly being used to understand political attitudes and behavior (e.g., Grimmer and Stewart, 2013; Roberts et al., 2014).

We then asked subjects to complete a set of political and demographic measures. This included traditional items such as party identification, ideology, political interest, a four-item political knowledge battery, and demographic characteristics. With the national sample, we also went on to assess attitudes toward the parties themselves in the form of feeling thermometers, as well as perceptions of the parties' ideological and political extremity at the mass and elite levels. This last set of items gauges multiple forms of partisan polarization, which we discuss in Section 4.

---

[7] Independent "leaners" are grouped with partisans in this table, following prior work (e.g., Bullock, 2011; Levendusky, 2010).

Our analysis proceeds in two main stages. We first consider the most frequently recurring terms in these open-ended responses and highlight commonalities across samples and subgroups. We then utilize machine learning to discover sets of words that tend to occur together, or *topics*, among subjects' responses, and we relate subjects' individual characteristics to their use of different topics.

3.3 2016 Results

We first examine the most frequent words across samples and subgroups.[8] Table 2 shows the most common words used to describe Democrats and Republicans, pooled across all three samples.[9] Many respondents correctly associated Democrats and Republicans with ideological orientations ("liberal" and "progressive" for Democrats; "conservative" for Republicans) and social groups (e.g., "young," "urban," "minorities" for Democrats; "old," "Southern," "white" for Republicans). Tables A.1 and A.2 in online Appendix A further show substantial consistency across the three samples, suggesting that different segments of the population share many partisan stereotypes. Likewise, we observe consistency across parties; four to six of the top ten terms used to describe Democrats and

Table 2 Most common stereotypes of Democrats and Republicans (2016 data)

	Stereotypes of Democrats	Stereotypes of Republicans
Most frequent response	Liberal (19.6%)	Conservative (14%)
2nd	Open-minded (4.2%)	Rich (7.6%)
3rd	Caring (3.9%)	White (5.2%)
4th	Youth (3.1%)	Prejudiced (3.9%)
5th	Smart (2.2%)	Senior citizens (3.7%)
6th	Poor (2.2%)	Ignorant (3.2%)
7th	Equality (2.1%)	Self interested (3.2%)
8th	Educated (2%)	Religious (3.1%)
9th	Minorities (1.8%)	Tradition (1.9%)
10th	Ignorant (1.7%)	Closed-minded (1.9%)

Source: Reprinted by permission from Springer Nature: Springer, *Political Behavior*, "Pigeonholing Partisans: Stereotypes of Party Supporters and Partisan Polarization," Jacob E. Rothschild et al., 2018.

---

[8] Given the novelty of these items, we also consider the structure of individuals' responses. Details are available in online Appendix A; in brief, the median number of words provided was four, and at least 96 percent of respondents provided answers to each stereotype question.

[9] Before constructing the summary tables, we recoded responses to group together words with highly similar meanings (e.g., "rich" and "wealthy"). The STM analyses are conducted using raw, non-recoded data.

Republicans appear across partisan subgroups (see Table 3). Both Democrats and Republicans associate Democrats with liberals, young people, minorities, and the poor, and Republicans with conservatives, whites, senior citizens, the religious, and the rich.

Answers diverge when it comes to terms with clear positive or negative valence. Respondents more often ascribe positive stereotypes to their own party and negative stereotypes to the other party. Democrats describe

Table 3 Stereotypes, by partisanship (national sample, 2016 data)

	Stereotypes of Democrats		**Stereotypes of Republicans**	
	Democratic Respondents	*Republican Respondents*	*Democratic Respondents*	*Republican Respondents*
Most frequent response	Liberal (16.7%)	Liberal (17.2%)	Conservative (12.4%)	Conservative (15.5%)
2nd	Caring (6.9%)	Ignorant (4.9%)	Rich (10.6%)	Rich (4.5%)
3rd	Open-minded (6.4%)	Poor (3.4%)	Prejudiced (6.8%)	Smart (3.8%)
4th	Equality (4.3%)	Lazy (3.2%)	White (5.7%)	Educated (3%)
5th	Smart (3.3%)	None (2.5%)	Ignorant (4.3%)	Honest (3%)
6th	Educated (2.6%)	Socialists (2.3%)	Closed-minded (3.2%)	Religious (2.4%)
7th	Minorities (2%)	Minorities (1.8%)	Self-interested (3.2%)	Individualist (2.3%)
8th	None (2%)	Unrealistic (1.8%)	Mean (2.4%)	Patriotism (2.1%)
9th	Middle-class (1.9%)	Social programs (1.5%)	None (2%)	White (2.1%)
10th	Poor (1.7%)	Abortion (1.4%)[10]	Religious (2%)	Middle-class (2%)

---

[10] The terms "dishonest" and "unions" were tied with abortion.

Table 4 Trait-based stereotypes (all samples)

	Democrats	**Republicans**
Most frequent response	Caring (8.6%)	Self-interested (5.6%)
2nd	Open-minded (7.5%)	Conservative (4.9%)
3rd	Liberal (6.7%)	Closed-minded (3.5%)
4th	Generous (2.7%)	Rigid (3.4%)
5th	Smart (2.7%)	Ignorant (3.1%)
6th	Ignorant (1.8%)	Mean (3.1%)
7th	Educated (1.6%)	Prejudiced (3%)
8th	Equality (1.5%)	Religious (2.6%)
9th	Friendly (1.4%)	Tradition (2.4%)
10th	None (1.4%)	Rich (2.2%)

copartisans as "caring" and "open-minded," while labeling Republicans as "prejudiced" and "closed-minded." Republicans see supporters of their party as "honest" and "individualist[ic]," while describing Democrats as "lazy" and "unrealistic." Identifiers with both parties also describe copartisans as "smart" and "educated," and outpartisans as "ignorant."

We thus see evidence of all three types of partisanship discussed in Section 2. Images of partisans include partisan-identity language and coalitional elements. While less prevalent, instrumental components also emerge – Republicans mention social programs and abortion when discussing Democrats, for example.

So far, this discussion has emphasized subjects' stereotypes in response to the most general prompt, but we also asked respondents to provide more focused stereotypes about partisans' traits, group memberships, and issue positions. These perceptions directly correspond to the partisan-identity, coalitional, and instrumental versions of partisanship that we laid out in Section 2. Tables 4, 5, and 6 indicate the top ten words listed about Republicans and Democrats for the traits, issues, and groups prompts; parallel tables broken out by respondents' partisanship can be found in online Appendix A. These tables indicate that people tend to have all three kinds of stereotypes concerning ordinary partisans.

Such a surface-level inspection of partisan stereotypes, while informative, is insufficiently systematic. To further minimize our assumptions, we evaluate subjects' responses using structural topic modeling (STM).[11] STM uses a form

---

[11] We use the "stm" package in R (Roberts, Stewart, & Tingley, 2017). For guidance in using this package, we rely on the information provided by Roberts et al. (2014) and Roberts, Stewart, and Airoldi (2016).

Table 5 Issue-based stereotypes (all samples)

	Democrats	Republicans
Most frequent response	Abortion (8%)	Taxes (10.9%)
2nd	Healthcare (7.5%)	Abortion (10.5%)
3rd	Social programs (6.2%)	Guns (7.7%)
4th	Environment (4.8%)	Immigration (7.2%)
5th	Education (4.6%)	National security (6.6%)
6th	Taxes (4.6%)	Religion (3.4%)
7th	Equality (4.3%)	Economy (3.4%)
8th	Guns (3.6%)	Rich (2.4%)
9th	Gay rights (3.5%)	Limited government (2.2%)
10th	Immigration (3.5%)	Healthcare (1.8%)

Table 6 Group-based stereotypes (all samples)

	Democrats	Republicans
Most frequent response	Blacks (5.8%)	Rich (10%)
2nd	Minorities (5.4%)	White (7.3%)
3rd	Women (4.2%)	Prejudiced (3.8%)
4th	Poor (4.2%)	Senior citizens (3.4%)
5th	Youth (3.7%)	Southern (2.7%)
6th	Students (3.6%)	Christians (2.6%)
7th	Latino (3%)	None (2.6%)
8th	Unions (3%)	Conservative (2.6%)
9th	Liberal (2.9%)	Men (2.2%)
10th	Middle-class (2.5%)	NRA (2.1%)

of machine learning to organize the words from a set of documents – here, the combined open-ended responses provided by each of our respondents – into topics based on the co-occurrence of individual words. In other words, STM provides a descriptive account of which terms appear together across respondents. Structural topic modeling thus allows researchers to "*discover* topics from the data, rather than assume them" (Roberts et al., 2014, 3). Given the paucity of work on stereotypes about mass-level partisans, such an approach suits our objectives well. Moreover, generating topics as lists of interrelated terms fits the nature of stereotypes themselves; social cognition research suggests that mental representations of social groups – or of any complex concept – consist of multiple elements or features that relate to each other in a structured way (Murphy & Medin, 1985; Stangor & Lange, 1994). Topics produced by the

Table 7 Democratic stereotype topics

Topic Number	FREX Words
1	poor, minor, left, wing, govern, liber, opinion
2	young, open, concern, forward, younger, passion, big
3	care, educ, intellig, generous, empathet, peopl, women
4	progress, urban, accept, right, liber, inclus, idealist
5	class, middl, divers, liber, think, free, american
6	blank, know, dont, none, concern, younger, forward
7	pro, choic, blue, union, collar, non, worker
8	smart, fair, equal, kind, support, help, compassion
9	lazi, liar, socialist, entitl, dishonest, self, black
10	mind, social, work, liber, open, justic, concern

Source: Reprinted by permission from Springer Nature: Springer, *Political Behavior*, "Pigeonholing Partisans: Stereotypes of Party Supporters and Partisan Polarization," Jacob E. Rothschild et al., 2018.

structural topic models should help us capture, as accurately as we can, the complex stereotypes people hold of party supporters.

Using this method, we generate stereotype topics for each party based on the responses across our pooled sample. Our structural topic model suggests ten coherent topics for both Democrats and Republicans.[12] Tables 7 and 8 present the themes that emerge from the STM analyses, along with words that uniquely and frequently define those themes (labeled FREX words in the technical language of STM).[13] These terms are "stemmed", i.e., trimmed down to the base of the word to combine words that have similar meanings but are different parts of speech (e.g., "loyalty" and "loyal," "intelligent" and "intelligence," "liberal" and "liberals"). This procedure is standard in text analysis.

As expected, topics for both parties exhibit a combination of terms referring to traits, social groups, and political issues. Many of the topics suggest that respondents attend both to the composition of the parties and to elite-level cues within their political and media environments. Not only do subjects tend to associate social groups and ideological labels with the appropriate party, but they also tend to get the issues correct. For instance, Democratic topics frequently mention groups such as minorities, women, and unions, while Republican topics include whites,

---

[12] While the appropriate number of topics cannot be objectively determined by the structural topic model, it provides metrics that researchers may use to determine a sensible quantity. See Rothschild et al. (2019) for more detail.

[13] Instead of reporting the most frequent terms found in each topic, we follow Roberts et al. (2014) in reporting words with the simplified frequency-exclusivity (FREX) scores. In simpler terms, these are words that frequently occur for a topic *and* not for other topics.

Table 8 Republican stereotype topics

Topic Number	FREX Words
1	blank, none, dont, know, money, self, fiscal
2	right, wing, trump, red, peopl, loud, money
3	white, southern, religi, uneduc, angri, money, fiscal
4	old, bigot, gun, fashion, anti, govern, know
5	busi, educ, wealthi, conserv, respons, male, valu
6	honest, patriot, strong, smart, work, independ, intellig
7	racist, rich, stupid, dumb, crazi, rude, sexist
8	close, mind, selfish, greedi, narrow, ignor, stubborn
9	conserv, tradit, money, fiscal, self, men, angri
10	pro, life, christian, class, older, middl, rural

Source: Reprinted by permission from Springer Nature: Springer, *Political Behavior*, "Pigeonholing Partisans: Stereotypes of Party Supporters and Partisan Polarization," Jacob E. Rothschild et al., 2018.

Southerners, and Christians. Also of note is that topics for both parties include a mix of positive and negative terms.

One important step is to refer to exemplar documents – responses that are most highly associated with each topic – to interpret the topics' meaning (Roberts et al. 2014). In our case, the exemplar documents indicate that the meanings of the topics match our broad interpretations of the FREX words. For example, the FREX words for topic 1 for Democrats seems to refer to the poor, racial minorities, and liberals. The exemplar texts – which include "poor, minority, liberal, government" and "liberal, left-wing, youth, people of color" – confirm this. The FREX words for topic 3 focus on prosocial personality traits, affirmed by exemplar responses like "caring, empathetic, generous, intelligent" and "thoughtful, open-minded, empathetic, intelligent." Topic 6 for Republicans includes ideas about honesty and patriotism; exemplar texts like "conservative, patriotic, loyal, honest" and "honest, strong, patriots, loyal" support this interpretation. Topic 3 emphasizes traditional demographics of the Republican Party, and exemplar statements like "white, conservative, Southern, bankers" and "white, Southern, Christian, gun owner" agree with this interpretation. We provide a list of exemplar documents in online Appendix A.

Following our orientation in Section 2 concerning partisan-identity, coalitional, and instrumental versions of partisanship, we next categorize each topic as predominantly about (1) traits, (2) groups, or (3) issues, or (4) as ambiguous. We do this by examining the FREX words within each topic. If no fewer than five of the top seven terms in a topic clearly deal with traits, groups, or issues, we label it accordingly; otherwise, we label the topic ambiguous. We reinforce these decisions by again looking at the ten exemplar documents most highly associated with each topic (provided in online Appendix A). This procedure produces an unexpected finding: group and issue topics never seem to occur independent of one another; the two types of partisanship appear linked in the minds of respondents. We therefore collapsed the issue and groups category into a single "issues and groups" heading. This process yields six trait topics, three group/issue topics, and nine ambiguous topics, plus the "don't know" topic for each party. Such coding practices follow the guidance of Roberts et al. (2014), who suggest that the substantive interpretation of topics falls ultimately to the researchers. Table 9 summarizes these groupings.[14] The exemplar documents for the topics categorized as traits include "closed-minded, stubborn, selfish, ignorant"; "smart, hardworking, conservative, compassionate"; and "fair, conscious, compassionate, informed." For the issues and groups topics, exemplars include "working-class, union members, gov't workers, blue-collar"; "business owners, rich middle class, older"; and "minorities, poor, urban, leftist." To further illustrate the common content of these types of topics, Figures 2 and 3 present word clouds for two traits topics and two issues/groups topics. These figures present the forty most frequent words for each, with larger words indicating more frequent terms.

Table 9 Topic categorization

Traits Topics	Issues and Groups Topics	Ambiguous Topics
Dem 2	Dem 1	Dem 4
Dem 3	Dem 7	Dem 5
Dem 8	Rep 10	Dem 9
Rep 6		Dem 10
Rep 7		Rep 2
Rep 8		Rep 3
		Rep 4
		Rep 5
		Rep 9
Total: 6	Total: 3	Total: 9

Note: "Don't know" topics are not categorized.
Source: Reprinted by permission from Springer Nature: Springer, *Political Behavior*, "Pigeonholing Partisans: Stereotypes of Party Supporters and Partisan Polarization," Jacob E. Rothschild et al., 2018.

---

[14] We use strict topic categorization standards, erring on the side of labeling a topic ambiguous any time the appropriate placement seemed unclear. As a robustness check, we also noted whether each ambiguous topic "leaned" toward traits or groups/issues; if we group these topics with the "unambiguous" topics, our substantive results remain largely unchanged.

Democrat Topic 3   ## Republican Topic 6

Figure 2 Traits topics

Democrat Topic 1   ## Republican Topic 10

Figure 3 Issues and groups topics

Not all types of topics prove equally common. Table 10 presents the aggregated frequency of terms from trait, group/issue, and ambiguous topics in our data. Trait-based terms prove considerably more common than groups and/or issues, and this holds across our different samples as well as partisan groups.[15] Although people of all party affiliations are more likely to mention traits than groups/issues, this seems especially true for Democrats, whose use of terms from the trait topics outweighs the groups/issues topics by more than a factor of two. However, words from ambiguous topics consistently outnumber those from the other categories, emphasizing that it is fairly uncommon for respondents to think

---

[15] Frequency is not a function of the number of topics in each category; a higher number of topics in one category does not imply higher usage by subjects.

Table 10 Proportions of kinds of stereotypes

	All Respondents	Democrats	Republicans	Independents[16]
Issues/ Groups	0.134	0.126	0.144	0.144
Traits	0.270	0.316	0.217	0.192
Ambiguous	0.480	0.476	0.521	0.404
Blank (R)	0.114	0.084	0.108	0.254
Blank (D)	0.119	0.080	0.129	0.266
Blank (both)	0.117	0.082	0.119	0.260

Source: Reprinted by permission from Springer Nature: Springer, *Political Behavior*, "Pigeonholing Partisans: Stereotypes of Party Supporters and Partisan Polarization," Jacob E. Rothschild et al., 2018.

of party supporters in only one way or another. For many, partisan stereotypes seem to be a combination of partisan-identity, instrumental, and coalitional ideas.

To investigate what demographic characteristics relate to these categories of stereotypes, we perform a series of OLS regressions with respondents' predicted topic proportions as our outcome variables.[17] We present the full model results in online Appendix A, highlighting what strike us as the most relevant results in Figure 4.[18] Political interest, political knowledge, and education all show a negative relationship with using the "don't know" topics. This comports with work on mental schemata of partisans, showing that political sophisticates more easily call images of the parties to mind (Baumer & Gold, 1995; Lodge & Hamill, 1986). Those more apt to engage with and learn about politics hold more concrete ideas about what partisans are like.

Political knowledge is also positively associated with responses from issue- or group-based topics (albeit weakly), perhaps indicating greater awareness of the policies and interests associated with the parties. Meanwhile, political interest relates to trait-based terms – individuals disposed to engage with politics may be more inclined to personalize partisan conflict. Education, meanwhile, has a negative relationship with trait-based topics. These variables thus appear to be

[16] Independents are pure independents only; leaners are grouped with partisans.
[17] We include dummy variables for each data collection to account for baseline differences between our samples. The results presented here are also robust to alternative specifications (e.g., beta regression).
[18] We include parallel analyses predicting use of each individual topic within the STM package. These can be found in Tables A.22 and A.23 in the online Appendix, which report when various respondent characteristics are related to specific topics. All independent and dependent variables are rescaled 0–1 for ease of interpretation.

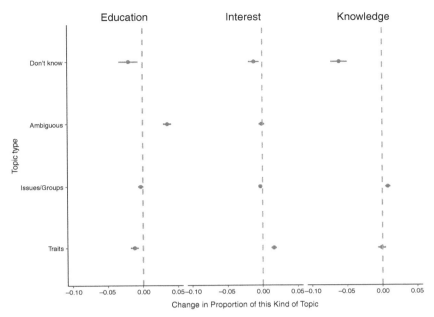

Figure 4 Relationships between sophistication and stereotype use
Source: Reprinted by permission from Springer Nature: Springer, *Political Behavior*, "Pigeonholing Partisans: Stereotypes of Party Supporters and Partisan Polarization," Jacob E. Rothschild et al., 2018.

associated with the content of partisan stereotypes, though in different ways. Interestingly, both measures of sophistication (i.e., knowledge and education) relate even more strongly to use of terms belonging to the "ambiguous" category; it may be that broader knowledge engenders more multifaceted stereotypes, whereas intensity of engagement with politics does not.[19]

The 2016 data provide a number of important findings. First, we find evidence that our method – asking respondents to list the words that come to mind when they think about typical party supporters – is a meaningful measure of partisan stereotypes. Responses are sensible, vary depending on the focus of the prompt, and relate to measures of political sophistication. This affirms the value of open-ended items to capture stereotype content when little previous empirical research exists. Second, these stereotypes contain themes connected to the partisan-identity, instrumental, and coalitional versions of partisanship. Partisan-identity stereotypes seem most common, although many respondents mix all three perspectives. The degree to

---

[19] We also find some differences in stereotype use among demographic groups. Most prominently, white and male respondents prove more likely to think of partisans in trait-based terms, a tendency previously found among privileged groups (Yzerbyt, Rocher, & Schadron, 1997). Full regression results predicting stereotype use can be found in Table A.21 in online Appendix A.

which respondents hold different stereotypes also varies depending on individuals' education, political interest, and political knowledge. In contemporary American politics, then, competing versions of partisanship exist, many people simultaneously hold ideas related to multiple types of partisanship, and individuals may emphasize disparate views of the parties based on context, intentional effort, or cues from elites.

3.4 2018 Design and Methods

Building on results from the 2016 data, we fielded a follow-up survey in the winter of 2018 using a nationally representative sample of the United States population. This survey focused directly on the three kinds of partisanship described in Section 2, asking specific questions about personality traits, issues, and groups. We thus rely on the 2018 data to look specifically at the partisan-identity, instrumental, and coalitional views of partisanship among the public, and to confirm that the conclusions we draw about stereotype content from the previous data are not simply a product of the political environment in 2016.

We worked with AmeriSpeak to administer this survey on a sample of 2,015 people. Funded and operated by NORC at the University of Chicago, AmeriSpeak is a probability-based panel designed to be representative of the US household population. Subjects were recruited in person, online, and by phone, after which they largely completed the survey online. Subjects without internet access participated by phone.[20] Table 11 gives a demographic breakdown of this sample, compared to the national sample from our 2016 data.

After agreeing to participate and answering demographic questions, respondents completed two tasks: open-ended items and checklist items about typical supporters of the Republican and Democratic Parties. Subjects were randomly assigned to complete both tasks with respect to one of the following attributes of Republicans and Democrats: "their personality and character traits," "political issues they find important," or "the social groups they belong to." These three areas correspond to the trait, issue, and group themes from the 2016 data and the three versions of partisanship discussed in Section 2. As an example, a respondent assigned to answer questions about traits would have been shown the following open-ended question.

"One way to understand supporters of the Democratic and Republican Parties is in terms of their personality and character traits. We are interested

---

[20] Randomly selected US households are sampled using area probability and address-based sampling, with a known, non-zero probability of selection from the NORC National Sample Frame. These sampled households are then contacted by US mail, telephone, and field interviewers (face to face). The panel provides sample coverage of approximately 97 percent of the US household population. AmeriSpeak panelists participate in NORC studies or studies conducted by NORC on behalf of governmental agencies, academic researchers, and media and commercial organizations. For more information, see AmeriSpeak.norc.org.

Table 11 Sample demographic characteristics (2018 data)

	Unweighted Percentage	
	2018 Sample	*2016 National Sample*
Female	52	52
Democrat	47	45
Independent[21]	18	18
Republican	35	37
Liberal	33	32
Moderate	32	31
Conservative	34	37
Nonwhite	36	20
	Unweighted Median	
Family Income ($)	50,000 to 60,000	50,000 to 75,000
Education	Some college, no degree	Bachelor's degree
Political Interest	3 out of 5	5 out of 7

in what traits come to mind when you think of people who typically support the [Democratic Party/Republican Party]. Picture in your mind the typical supporter of the [Democratic Party/Republican Party]. In a few sentences, how would you describe this person in terms of their traits?"

That question was asked about both kinds of partisans (order randomized) and was followed by a checklist item, described to them as follows.

"Now we are interested in whether you think the specific traits below are typical of people who support the [Democratic Party/Republican Party]. For the list of traits below, please check which traits you think are typical of supporters of the [Democratic Party/Republican Party]."

Items on each checklist came from the top-ten lists we generated from the corresponding questions in the 2016 data. We supplemented these with a few additional terms to ensure the lists were relatively balanced with positive and negative terms and contained items that could be applied to both Republicans and Democrats. This helps avoid confounding between affective charge and the three types of stereotypes we emphasize throughout this Element. Table 12 shows the checklist items for the three different areas.

As with the 2016 data, we use structural topic models to uncover broad themes present in the 2018 open-ended responses. The checklists then distill the most common partisan stereotypes in a simpler form, enabling us to look at the degree of consensus among the American public. These different procedures, as

---

[21] These are, again, pure independents, with leaners treated as partisans.

Table 12 Checklist items

Personality/Character Traits	**Political Issues**	**Social Groups**
Caring	Environment	African Americans
Open-minded	Education	Women
Generous	Healthcare	The poor
Honest	Social Security	Latinos/Hispanics
Patriotic	LGBT rights	The middle class
Individualistic	Racial equality	LGBT
Hardworking	Taxes	Immigrants
Idealistic	National security	Blue-collar workers
Selfish	Budget deficit	Gun owners
Elitist	Crime	Men
Mean	Business regulations	Christians
Hypocritical	Foreign affairs	Senior citizens
Prejudiced	Guns	Whites
Lazy	Immigration	The wealthy
Rigid	Abortion	Young people

mentioned, follow the common sequence of research on the content of stereo-types in social psychology research (e.g., Katz & Braly, 1933; Gilbert, 1951; Stangor & Lange, 1994; Madon, 1997; Madon et al., 2001), and they provide us with an understanding of partisan stereotypes that is both broad and deep.

3.5 2018 Results

To explore stereotype content in the 2018 data, we turn to two descriptive analyses: (1) an STM using the open-ended responses and (2) a comparison of which items respondents chose for the checklist tasks.[22] Unlike with the 2016 data, we do not present top-ten lists from the open-ended items. The format of these questions (one large text box soliciting responses in sentence form, instead of asking for four specific words) means that a list of the most common words inevitably contains mundane words such as "public," "want," and "can." While this structure is well suited to understanding people's unstructured ideas, and the causal questions we consider in Section 4, looking at the most common words also becomes a less helpful exercise. Interested readers can find tables of these in online Appendix A.

---

[22] Details on the structure of responses are available in online Appendix A. In brief, about 85 percent of respondents answered the open-ended items, and most provided responses of reasonable length. At least 96 percent chose one or more of the checklist items for each party; most chose five to eight options, depending on the domain. Few selected all or nearly all fifteen boxes, suggesting most respondents differentiate between the parties.

Our STM procedure generated models with nine topics for Republicans and nine topics for Democrats.[23] The full list of topics appears in Tables 13 and 14. As expected, some topics touch on traits, others on issues, and others on groups, indicating that people completed these tasks as instructed. In addition, these results give support for the partisan-identity, instrumental, and coalitional views of partisans. For example, topics 2 and 3 for Democrats clearly correspond to issue priorities among partisans. Topic 7 for Democrats and topic 5 for Republicans focus on coalitional or group-based distinctions. Topic 4 for Republicans and topic 1 for Democrats cover partisan-identity or trait-based

Table 13 Democratic stereotype topics (2018 data)

Topic Number	FREX Words
1	want, help, peopl, money, need, hard, everyon
2	healthcar, women, right, issu, program, social, wage
3	health, import, care, freedom, support, individu, well
4	republican, parti, democrat, just, time, interest, usual
5	gun, pro, control, believ, free, choic, anti
6	mind, liber, open, accept, think, open-mind, view
7	group, belong, minor, organ, colleg, union, like
8	class, middl, lower, incom, low, poor, understand
9	dont, everyth, will, seem, make, govern, countri

Table 14 Republican stereotype topics (2018 data)

Topic Number	FREX Words
1	work, govern, hard, constitut, strong, live, respons
2	republican, parti, democrat, typic, issu, import, tend
3	rich, class, upper, middl, close, racist, old
4	dont, know, think, selfish, polit, self, see
5	nra, group, belong, club, church, older, like
6	fear, chang, believ, religi, financi, accept, major
7	immigr, tax, abort, secur, regul, concern, economi
8	care, help, peopl, need, good, make, take
9	often, right, conserv, mani, doesnt, much, common

---

[23] Note that the topic models incorporated baseline differences in topic use depending on whether subjects were asked about groups, issues, or traits.

views of the parties. These findings suggest that elements of all three forms of partisan stereotypes exist in subjects' minds and that they can recall them when prompted. This supports our view of partisanship from Section 2 and confirms our 2016 findings. Moreover, these results validate the prompts we used to generate the text responses – people seem to be taking them as intended.

The checklist items provide further insight into Americans' stereotypes of Republicans and Democrats, including novel information not present in our earlier data. Figures 5, 6, and 7 show results for the traits, issues, and groups checklists. The figures display a difference score between the two parties – that is, how much more or less a term was selected to describe Democrats over Republicans. Negative values on these graphs indicate that a word was more frequently associated with Republicans, while positive values show that the item was more often connected to Democrats. Words around the zero mark of the graph were about equally ascribed to Democrats and Republicans. These figures also break out the estimates by partisanship, given the likely influence of partisan identity on stereotype content.[24]

Figure 5 displays a stark difference between partisans concerning traits they associate with each party. Generally, this follows an unsurprising pattern, with partisans associating more positive traits (e.g., honest, generous, open-minded) with their own side, and more negative traits (e.g., elitist, mean, prejudiced) with their opponents. Exceptions exist – all partisan groups associate idealism more with Democrats and individualism more with Republicans – but trait-based stereotypes of typical partisans seem heavily influenced by individuals' own party attachments. They appear motivated to maintain an overall positive image of the inparty and a negative image of the outparty, just as social identity theory (Tajfel & Turner, 1979), as well as research on trait ownership (e.g., Goggin & Theodoridis, 2017; Hayes, 2005), would predict.

Figure 6 shows this same breakdown for the issues checklist. Recall that these items asked subjects to indicate which issues partisans in the electorate cared about, not the ideological positions of the parties in these areas. Here, we see more agreement between partisans about which issues are important to Democrats and Republicans. Republicans, Democrats, and independents all associate LGBT rights, the environment, and racial equality with typical Democrats. National security, taxes, business regulations, and guns are similarly linked to typical Republicans. This finding coheres well with research on party reputations (e.g., Pope & Woon, 2009; Goggin & Theodoridis, 2017).

---

[24] Parallel figures for the entire sample and broken out by political interest are in online Appendix A.

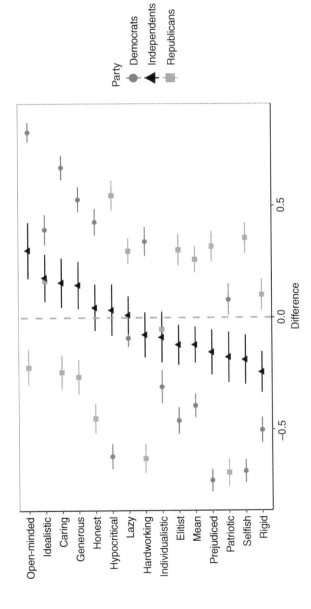

Figure 5 Checklist items – traits, partisan subsets (2018 data)

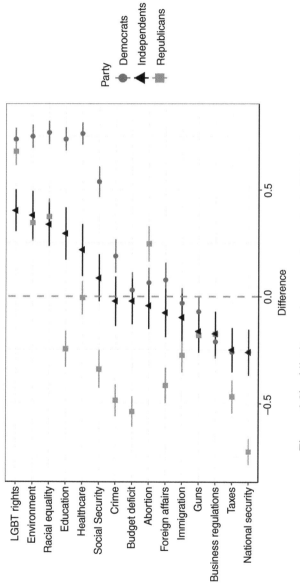

Figure 6 Checklist items – issues, partisan subsets (2018 data)

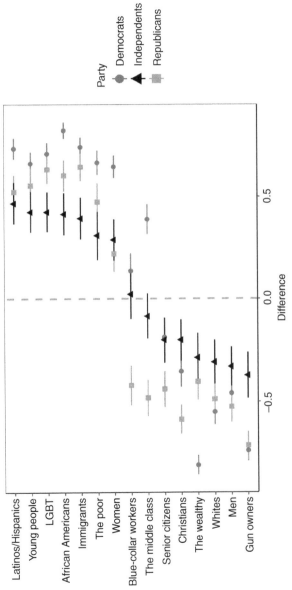

Figure 7 Checklist items – groups, partisan subsets (2018 data)

A number of issues, however, see less consensus among respondents. These include education, social security, crime, budget deficits, and foreign affairs. On these items, partisans perceive that supporters of their own party place more emphasis on these issues than their opponents do. This may be due to the wider appeal of these issues, or because they are generally seen as more important than other policies; further work should examine these possibilities.

Figure 7 shows distributions for the group-focused checklist items, and here we see even more agreement. Regardless of subjects' own party attachments, Latinos, young people, LGBT individuals, African Americans, the poor, immigrants, and women are all associated more with Democrats. Senior citizens, Christians, the wealthy, whites, gun owners, and men are all associated more with Republicans. For a number of these groups, Republican and Democratic respondents exhibit minimal differences in their perceptions. Only two groups seem to divide subjects: blue-collar workers and the middle class. Partisans attribute these groups more to copartisans than to their outparty, likely due to the positive framing both receive in American political discourse.

3.6 Conclusions

In this section, we discussed two novel sources of survey data concerning the stereotypes individuals have of ordinary partisans. The 2016 survey presented subjects with open-ended questions, asking them to list the words that came to their minds regarding typical Republican and Democratic Party supporters. The 2018 data built on this method, asking subjects for their open-ended thoughts on partisans in the specific areas of traits, issues, and groups, as well as gauging partisan stereotypes through the use of targeted checklist tasks. These data sources provide a rich and detailed view into Americans' partisan stereotypes.

From both surveys, a number of important patterns emerge. First, respondents provide meaningful answers when prompted to report their stereotypes of Republicans and Democrats, be they general or specific. People hold mental images of both kinds of partisans in their heads and seem to have little difficulty expressing them. Stereotypes of all kinds also seem to involve affectively charged terms and more emotionally neutral descriptions. While Americans continue to lack much ideological content in their political views (Converse, 1964; Kinder & Kalmoe, 2017), they seem to recognize it in partisans at least in a superficial way.

Second, there is considerable agreement about what Republican and Democratic supporters are like. Trait, issue, and group-based language emerges to describe both kinds of partisans, supporting the partisan-identity, instrumental, and coalitional views of partisanship discussed in Section 2. Republicans,

Democrats, and independents also express these stereotypes in similar amounts, suggesting a good deal of cross-partisan consensus. When it comes to closed-ended measures of stereotypes, Republicans and Democrats have similar views concerning the issues and groups linked to partisans from both sides.

Third, important distinctions arise between trait-based and other elements of partisan stereotypes. In the 2016 data, we found that trait-based themes were more common than group- and issue-focused topics. Given the current political context, which has seen partisanship become a personalized aspect of people's social lives, partisan-identity and trait-based differences between the parties may be more commonly thought about than other attributes. Considering the checklist items from 2018, we see another interesting pattern: partisans are deeply divided on trait-based evaluations of the parties but show a striking amount of consensus when discussing the groups and issues connected to Republicans and Democrats. It may be that traits are more linked to a polarized, divisive view of the parties than to more instrumental or coalitional versions of partisanship, and that personalization of partisanship is partly to blame for the present intensity of partisan conflict in both social and political domains.

The results in this section, though, can say little about the causal processes that underlie this last suggestion. We have taken an intentionally descriptive approach, seeking to document the stereotypes as they exist in the American public. While sorely needed in this area, such an approach renders our results and analyses severely limited in the domain of causal inference.

Such causal work cannot be casually swept under the rug. Having documented the stereotypes that exist, how does holding different forms of partisan stereotypes relate to polarization? Do stereotypes of different kinds have the potential to polarize or depolarize the electorate? Or are Americans' perceptions of the parties too firmly established to respond to shifts in the underlying stereotypes? We turn to these questions next.

4 Party Images and Partisan Polarization

In the spring of 2016, at the tail end of that year's presidential primaries, a woman stranded in a broken-down vehicle on the North Carolina stretch of I-26 called for roadside assistance. A tow truck arrived on the scene, and the driver – Kenneth Shupe, a fifty-one-year-old conservative Christian from South Carolina – began connecting the truck's towing apparatus to the woman's immobilized Toyota. Walking around the rear of the car, the truck driver spotted a Bernie Sanders bumper sticker and abruptly aborted the service he had just begun to render. "Every business dealing in recent history that I've had with a socialist minded person, I haven't gotten paid," Shupe later explained (Larimer, 2016). In effect, Shupe was relying on a *stereotype* of Sanders supporters – that they could not be trusted to pay their fair share (and, in this case, their towing bills). Perhaps this stereotype was rooted in Shupe's anecdotal experience; perhaps it was the product of media portrayals. In any case, it clearly influenced his behavior.

Is Shupe's behavior unusual? What are the larger consequences of the images people have of typical party supporters? In Section 3, we presented manifestations of the instrumental, coalitional, and identity-based views in Americans' stereotypes of rank-and-file partisans. Thus far, our effort has centered on establishing the substantive content of party stereotypes. Interesting as this content may be on its own, our justification for engaging in this work ultimately rests on the assumption that it significantly influences American political attitudes and behavior. What, if anything, are the *consequences* of these stereotypes?

One man's political stereotypes may influence his personal willingness to render a service, but are people's images of ordinary Democrats and Republicans politically meaningful in a broader sense? What is the relationship between these stereotypes and political conflict? Are stereotypes of the partisan rank-and-file an end product of polarization, or do they contribute to it? Do they universally exacerbate partisan conflict, or does one kind of stereotype offer a way to temper partisan divides in the contemporary United States?

We draw on observational and experimental survey data to explore the relationships between different types of party images and a variety of outcomes related to polarization. We first return to the observational data from 2016 (also see Rothschild et al., 2019). Extrapolating from our structural topic model analyses, we connect respondents' predominantly trait-based terms, compared to terms centered around issues or groups, to measures of affective and ideological polarization. Here we find that the use of traits is associated with greater polarization (and perceived polarization) across all of our dependent variables. Terms from issue- or group-based topics, meanwhile, show virtually no relationships. From this, we conclude that partisan-identity stereotypes go hand-in-hand with polarization.

To ascertain the causal nature of this relationship, we leverage an experimental manipulation in our 2018 data. The survey experiment prompted subjects to think about mass-level partisans in terms of their traits, the issues they find important, or the groups to which they belong. Subjects were randomly assigned to complete one of these three tasks, or no task at all. We find that prompting individuals to think of partisans in terms of political issues decreases personal and perceived polarization (both affective and ideological) compared to the traits, groups, and control conditions. Respondents in the traits and control conditions, meanwhile, exhibit similar levels of polarization – sensible given that trait-based stereotypes appear most common among the public. In other words, because a large proportion of Americans are already prone to think of party supporters in partisan-identity terms, we observe a high baseline of polarization. If those people can instead be induced to think of the parties in terms of political issues, polarization on a number of dimensions may be ameliorated.

Our analyses show the content of party images to be highly consequential for political attitudes among the American public. Thinking of ordinary partisans in terms of their personal traits (i.e., in a manner consistent with partisanship as a social identity) or the other groups associated with the parties results in higher levels of polarization, while thinking instead about the political issues partisans find important decreases polarization. We find cause for optimism in these results; reducing polarization does not require people to pretend that partisans all agree with one another – a daunting and ultimately undesirable proposition in today's political environment. Instead, perceptions of the *root* of those divisions push people toward more or less partisan conflict, and prompting them to focus on certain sources of that conflict over others may actually diminish its intensity.

4.1 Party Images and Their Consequences

Given their importance to the American political process, one might expect to find an expansive literature documenting people's images of the parties (broadly), stereotypes of partisans (more specifically), and the consequences of these mental representations for political behavior. A few notable efforts along these lines, as noted in Section 2, do exist. By and large, however, few studies have looked beyond the mere descriptive content of these stereotypes to consider their political impact.

Those that do so present a mixed picture of the consequences of people's images of parties and partisans. One stream of research observes that stereotypes of the parties help citizens form their own positions on political issues, decide which party to identify with, and evaluate candidates (Conover & Feldman, 1989; Geer, 1991; Rahn, 1993; Rahn & Cramer, 1996; Green, Palmquist, & Schickler, 2002). From this perspective, stereotypes of the parties can serve as useful cues when citizens make decisions in an increasingly complex information environment.

On the other hand, these stereotypes may create difficulties for politicians. Stereotypes of the parties involve ownership over issues, personality traits, and even assumptions about gender (Petrocik, 1996; Hayes, 2005; Winter, 2010). As a result, candidates may pay a price if they violate these mental images and go against the issue positions, attributes, and gender expectations connected to their party (Bauer, Yong, & Krupnikov, 2017; Cassese & Holman, 2018; Severson, 2018; Bauer, 2019). Party-related stereotypes thus may simplify the political landscape for voters, but at the same time restrict the flexibility of candidates and elected officials. Furthermore, holding inaccurate or exaggerated stereotypes can increase affective and ideological polarization, along with other negative attitudes toward opposing partisans (Ahler & Sood, 2018).

As a whole, existing work on stereotypes of the parties suggests there are costs and benefits to such mental shortcuts. However, only a small handful of studies in this area explicitly consider links between stereotypes and polarization (Ahler & Sood, 2018), and none directly consider stereotypes of rank-and-file partisans (as opposed to candidates or the parties as organizations). The link between mental images of ordinary partisans and partisan conflict, and the potential of some stereotypes to reduce polarization, therefore remains unknown.

4.2 Stereotypes and Social Behavior

For theoretical guidance on this point, we turn to more general research on stereotypes and their influence. Given the broad power of stereotypes to exacerbate intergroup conflict, partisan stereotypes in particular may have the potential to magnify partisan polarization. We draw on work from various fields in the social sciences and echo the discussion in Section 2, where this logic is laid out in more detail.

While stereotypes provide people with mental shortcuts that help them to navigate complex social environments, they also influence a host of mental processes and can have detrimental effects on attitudes and behavior (Lippmann, 1922; Allport, 1954; Macrae & Bodenhausen, 2000). For example, they can cause people to focus attention and memory on how much an individual or object supports or challenges their preexisting views (Stangor & McMillan, 1992; Macrae & Bodenhausen, 2000). Stereotypes also shift the standards by which people evaluate others and can increase hostility and interpersonal conflict (Chen & Bargh, 1997). As a result, what people remember and notice about their partisan friends, neighbors, and coworkers may depend on the mental images people have about rank-and-file Republicans and Democrats.

Stereotypes can influence what people do in addition to what they think. Early research in this area found that subtly priming stereotypes caused individuals to behave in ways consistent with those generalizations (Bargh, Chen, & Burrows, 1996). Later research found that this kind of stereotype priming could change how people reacted to stereotype-relevant groups (Cesario, Plaks, & Higgins, 2006). Although there has been some controversy about the robustness of these effects (Doyen et al., 2012; Harris et al., 2013), recent meta-analyses confirm that this type of priming has modest, but reliable, effects on behavior (Weingarten et al., 2016). Messages from the media, candidates, and other sources about partisans may thus prime different stereotypes and then influence Americans' behavior toward ordinary Republicans and Democrats.

4.3 Expectations

To predict the influence of different types of partisan stereotypes, we refer to the theoretical foundation discussed in Section 2. The more individuals consider party affiliation to be an identity in itself, the more they should view partisan groups as homogeneous (Hogg, 1992), and the more they should be inclined to make trait-based attributions to partisans (Hamilton & Sherman, 1996). From this perspective, partisans represent fundamentally different classes of people with sharp divisions based on inherent traits, rather than people who simply have differences of opinion (Haslam, Rothschild, & Ernst, 2000). Moreover, while most stereotypes carry some degree of affective charge (Jackson et al., 1997; Fiske et al., 2002), trait stereotypes tend to express an affective component most explicitly. Individuals with this mindset should, therefore, be motivated to accentuate differences between their own party and the outparty (Abrams & Hogg, 1988; Tajfel & Turner, 1979), increasing both affective and ideological polarization.

In contrast, stereotypes that focus on partisans' issue positions – linked to the instrumental view of partisanship – reorient differences to be less about intrinsic divides between people and more about different perspectives and priorities. Focusing on issue-based stereotypes also requires people to engage in some amount of perspective-taking; they must be able to envision what other people think is important and what different partisans believe. This way of thinking has been linked to lower amounts of prejudice, implicit bias, and intergroup conflict (Galinsky & Moskowitz, 2000; Todd et al., 2011). As a result, issue-based stereotypes should be associated with lower amounts of affective and ideological polarization.[25]

---

[25] This latter expectation may seem to some degree counterintuitive. However, as noted by Converse (1964), many if not most members of the public tend not to link discrete policies with an overarching ideological belief system. Instead, ideology *per se* typically functions as a symbolic label, fostering partisan division in a way that policy priorities likely do not (see, e.g., Webster & Abramowitz, 2017). Moreover, Clifford (2020) links both partisan and ideological

Group-based stereotypes, which we connect to the coalitional view of partisanship, should have a less consistent connection to polarization. They likely prime various identities like religion, class, and race, which could go on to exacerbate partisan conflict. On the other hand, group stereotypes also may emphasize the fact that people belong to some, but not all, of the groups connected to the parties. This kind of cross-pressuring has the potential to reduce polarization and extremism (Berelson, Lazarsfeld, & McPhee, 1954; Brader, Tucker, & Therriault, 2014). Group-focused images of the parties may also cue norms about those groups (e.g., religious tolerance, racial egalitarianism, anti-sexism), which then weaken the polarizing potential of such stereotypes. Coalitional stereotypes, then, fall between the instrumental and partisan-identity views.

These predictions can be restated in the following hypotheses.

H1: *Trait-based thinking about partisanship will lead to greater partisan polarization relative to an emphasis on groups or issues.*

H2: *Issue-based stereotypes will lead to lower polarization compared to other kinds of stereotypes.*

H3: *Group-focused stereotypes will lead to more moderate amounts of polarization that fall somewhere between issue-based and trait-based stereotypes.*

We turn now to our tests of these hypotheses, which come both from observational and experimental data about stereotypes of ordinary partisans.

4.4 Evidence from an Observational Study

We first evaluate these three hypotheses by assessing the correlations between different kinds of partisan stereotypes and polarization. Having shown in previous sections that people's top-of-the-head stereotypes of Democrats and Republicans tend to deal mainly with political issues, social groups, or individual traits, we now explore how these different mental images relate to important political variables.

4.4.1 Data and Methods

We draw on data described in Section 3 – the nationally diverse data collected via Research Now (N = 861) in August 2016. The key elements included in the survey are open-ended measures of respondents' stereotypes and items gauging polarization in various forms. We used the open-ended items to elicit people's stereotypes of ordinary Democrats and Republicans and analyzed these responses using structural topic modeling (STM). Recall that the STM procedure detailed in Section 3 generated numeric topic proportions ranging from 0 to 1 for each topic across all respondents, with this value corresponding to the

labels to trait inferences about mass partisans' moral character, again suggesting that trait-based stereotypes may exacerbate ideological polarization.

proportion of their response associated with a given topic. We categorized each topic as referring primarily to traits, referring primarily to political issues and social groups, or "ambiguous." This allowed us to generate summary values describing the proportion of respondents' stereotypes that referred to traits, issues, groups, or other ideas.

The Research Now data also incorporated several measures of partisan polarization. We assessed subjects' views of the extremity and ideological positioning of partisans both in the mass public and in Congress; respondents' own ideological self-placement; and affective polarization, operationalized as the absolute difference of feeling thermometer evaluations of the Democratic and Republican Parties. To understand the relationship between certain kinds of partisan stereotypes and these different forms of polarization, we regressed these variables on the topic proportions. Details about the specific measures described in the previous paragraph, as well as the process by which we generated the topic proportions, are available in online Appendix B.

4.4.2 Results

A first look using observational data suggests that partisan stereotype content does have a significant relationship with other politically important attitudes and behaviors. These findings are summarized in Figure 8. We pool Democratic and Republican respondents here; see online Appendix B for figures that break down results by respondent partisanship.

We begin by considering the relationship between partisan stereotypes and ideological polarization. Thinking about rank-and-file Democrats and Republicans in terms of political issues or social groups does not significantly relate to perceptions of ideological distance between the parties. However, conceiving of party supporters in terms of *traits* relates to a substantial, statistically significant increase in perceived ideological distance between the parties at both the mass and the elite level. In other words, holding trait-centered stereotypes correlates strongly with greater perceived ideological polarization. Moreover, respondents who express larger proportions of terms from trait-based topics tend to be more ideologically extreme themselves (as measured with a folded version of the traditional seven-point ideology scale).

We also find that trait-centered party stereotypes have a significant positive relationship with affective polarization, measured as the absolute difference between respondents' feeling thermometer evaluations of the parties (see Iyengar, Sood, & Lelkes, 2012; Mason, 2015). Those who personalize partisanship or conceive of party affiliation in partisan-identity terms exhibit more strongly positive evaluations of their inparty and/or more negative assessments of the outparty.

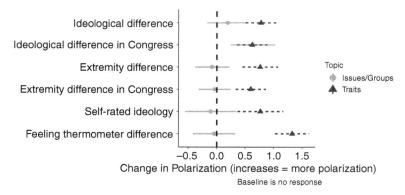

Figure 8 Partisan stereotypes and polarization, observational analyses
Source: Adapted by permission from Springer Nature: Springer, *Political Behavior*, "Pigeonholing Partisans: Stereotypes of Party Supporters and Partisan Polarization," Jacob E. Rothschild et al., 2018.

Thinking of the parties in terms of political issues or social groups has no such relationship.

This pattern of results proves robust in two important ways. First, we control for the average valence respondents attached to the open-ended stereotype responses they provided.[26] Including this valence measure allows us to separate the affective charge of these terms from their substantive content. In fact, valence alone does not have a significant relationship with polarization when included alongside measures of stereotype content; the substantive nature of people's images of the parties matters far more than the simple positivity or negativity attached to these images. This suggests, importantly, that the use of trait-based stereotypes is not merely an expression of interparty affect (i.e., the attribution of positive traits to the inparty and negative traits to the outparty); indeed, many of the trait words in our data carry only mild affective charges. Second, we note that these results do not depend on our use of STM or on the categorization procedure explained in Section 3. When we use a dictionary-based recoding method to generate topic proportions, we observe the same pattern of results. Net of valence, trait-based stereotypes have a positive, significant relationship with polarization, but issue- and group-based stereotypes do not. (See online Appendix B for more details on this alternative method.)

---

[26] Subjects were asked to rate each of the responses they provided "on a scale from negative (1) to positive (7)."

4.5 Evaluating the Causal Link

The observational data described above suggest a close connection between partisan stereotype content and polarization. However, these results do not allow us to draw conclusions about the direction of this relationship; do stereotypes influence polarization, or does polarization alter stereotype content? Nor do they preclude the possibility that some unobserved factors are really influencing *both* stereotype content and polarization (such as exposure to specific kinds of media messages about partisans). To circumvent these short-comings, we turn to an experimental manipulation of stereotypes of ordinary partisans. An experimental approach allows us to dismiss both of these concerns; the temporal ordering of the treatment and outcome measures rules out the possibility of reverse causality, and random assignment obviates unobserved confounding variables. We can say with confidence that any relationship we observe between partisan stereotype content and polarization as a result of our experimental manipulations is a causal one.

Our attempt to pin down the causal relationship between partisan stereotype content and polarization involved two survey experiments conducted in the spring and summer of 2018, both using the same treatments. To help envision these treatments, recall the thought experiment from Section 2 which asked you to conjure up images of typical Democrats and Republicans. Would your answers have been different if we first nudged you to think about the ways partisans might differ in terms of their fundamental personality or character traits? What if we had encouraged you to believe that the primary wedge between Democrats and Republicans is a difference in opinion on political issues? Beyond that, do these subtle shifts in thinking do more than move stereotypes and go on to influence polarization more broadly? We implement this kind of task in the experiments outlined below. We first describe our samples and experimental procedure and then summarize our results.

4.5.1 Data and Methods

We conducted two survey experiments on different populations. Study 1, fielded in March and April of 2018, utilized a convenience sample of 268 undergraduates at a large Midwestern university (details on sample recruitment are available in online Appendix B). While not representative of the population of the United States, this kind of convenience sample can still provide valid causal inferences and insights into our hypotheses (Druckman & Kam, 2011). Study 2 was embedded in the 2018 survey discussed in Section 3, which involved a nationally representative probability sample of US adults fielded during November and December of that year. Further details on this sample are

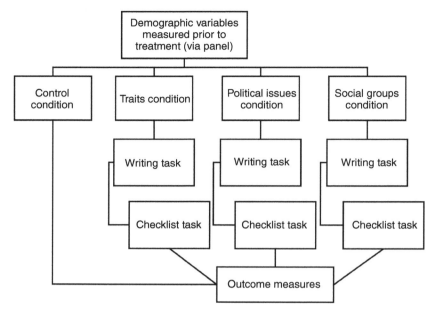

Figure 9 Experimental flow

available in online Appendix B. This second experiment serves to confirm the first while bolstering the generalizability of our findings. The demographic characteristics for both samples are summarized in Table 15.

The procedure was the same across both samples, and the experimental logic is summarized in Figure 9. We assigned respondents to one of four treatment conditions. The first three conditions were designed to prime the different kinds of mass-level partisan stereotypes identified in Section 3 – traits, social group memberships, or political issues. Each respondent completed two tasks related to the condition to which they were assigned, which together served as a single treatment.

The first task asked subjects to write two short paragraphs – one describing a typical Democratic Party supporter, the other a typical Republican Party supporter – in terms of their individual traits, the social groups they belong to, or the political issues they find important. In order to enhance engagement with the treatments – and to ensure that subjects are "complying" and thinking about partisans along the lines we intended – a second task presented respondents with two fifteen-item checklists corresponding to traits, groups, or political issues, and asked them to select the items which describe a typical Democratic Party supporter and a typical Republican Party supporter (see Table 12). This approach follows a good deal of research on stereotyping, going back to the

Table 15 Sample demographic characteristics

	Student Sample	Probability Sample
Percent Female	49.1%	51.7%
Percent White	47.8%	63.7%
Percent Democratic (with leaners)	83.4%	47.1%
Percent Republican (with leaners)	10.8%	35.0%
Percent Independent	5.8%	17.8%
Median Household Income ($)	150,000 to 199,999	50,000 to 59,999
Median Age	20	49
N	268	2,015

Note: The table contains unweighted estimates.

earliest such efforts (e.g., Katz & Braly, 1933). Subjects completed these tasks one at a time, considering first one party and then the other. The order in which the parties were presented was randomized across respondents but held constant across the two tasks for each individual. A fourth group, the control, did not complete any of these tasks and instead proceeded directly to the outcome measures.

Respondents then answered a set of items that tap various forms of polarization, which include a range of questions used in existing research. These include feeling thermometers for each party, with affective polarization operationalized as the absolute difference between the two; a folded version of the standard seven-point liberal–conservative ideology scale to measure respondents' own ideological extremity; and items capturing respondents' perceptions of mass-level Democrats and Republicans' ideological positions, as well as those of Democrats and Republicans in Congress. Differentials between the parties on these latter items measure respondents' perceptions of ideological distance between the parties at the mass and elite levels. Subjects also answered an item measuring their sense of partisan social identity (see Huddy, Mason, & Aarøe, 2015). Finally, the survey asked two questions assessing preferences for social distance between the parties: whether respondents would be upset if a family member dated a member of the outparty (adapted from Iyengar, Sood, & Lelkes, 2012) and whether it is appropriate to block or defriend someone on social media for political reasons. Full wordings for the treatments and other items can be found in online Appendix B.

4.5.2 Study 1 Results

We first examine results from the undergraduate convenience sample. Overall, the results provide support for our hypotheses and more generally suggest that our treatments work as intended, stimulating different forms of thinking about ordinary partisans. Details on treatment effects for our different outcome variables follow below. All hypothesis tests comparing treatment conditions are two-tailed unless noted otherwise.

Figure 10 presents results for our primary measures of affective polarization (feeling thermometer differences between the parties) and ideological polarization (self-rated ideological extremity, i.e., a folded version of the seven-point ideology scale where higher values indicate more extreme views). We see suggestive evidence for the expected effect on polarization of both types. The left-hand panel of Figure 10 shows that thinking of mass partisans in identity-based terms seems to exert a small effect on affective polarization; subjects in the "traits" condition show slightly larger feeling thermometer differentials. However, this difference does not reach statistical significance ($p = 0.56$). The same pattern is evident concerning measures of respondents' own ideological extremity in the second panel; those in

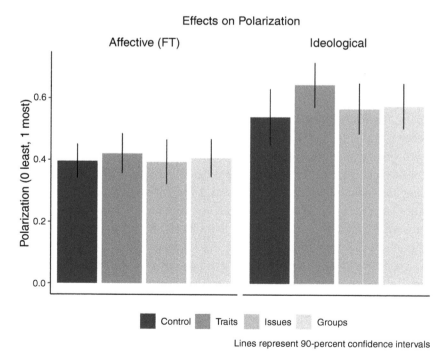

Figure 10 Treatment effects on polarization (undergraduate sample)

the traits condition show markedly higher levels of ideological polarization than those in the other treatment groups, and this difference approaches conventional levels of statistical significance (p = 0.08). The groups and issues conditions, though both somewhat higher than the control, show no significant differences.

Figure 11 presents treatment effects on perceptions of ideological polarization, among mass-level partisans and partisans in Congress. In the former case (first panel), we see no significant difference between the "traits" group and the control condition. However, contrary to our expectations, the "groups" treatment seems to prompt greater perceptions of ideological distance between party supporters, relative to both the control (p = 0.06) and "traits" (p = 0.04). A similar pattern emerges with respect to perceived ideological differences between partisans in Congress (second panel); the "groups" treatment shows a significant positive effect (p = 0.06) compared to "traits". Though this effect was not expected, it does support our more general notion that thinking of mass partisans in different stereotypic terms may lead to different attitudes and perceptions of polarization.

We turn next to measures of social distance between partisans, presented in Figure 12. In the first panel, we see evidence that thinking of partisans in social

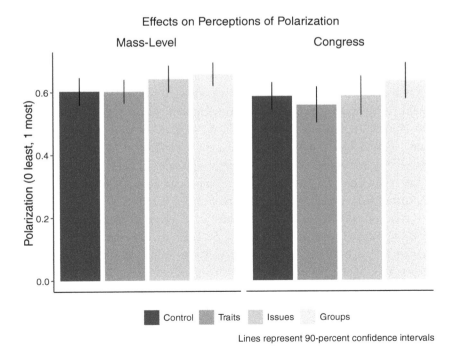

Figure 11 Treatment effects on perceptions of ideological polarization
(undergraduate sample)

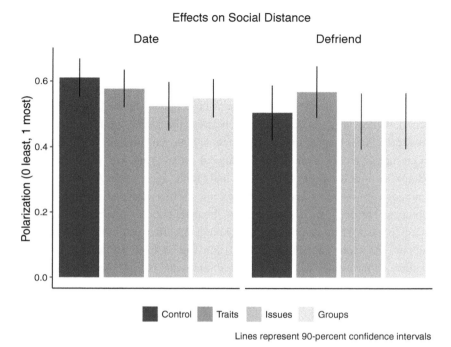

Figure 12 Treatment effects on partisan social distance (undergraduate sample)

identity (i.e., trait-based) terms results in greater social distance. Those in the "traits" treatment do not prove significantly more likely to express displeasure about a family member dating a supporter of the opposing party, relative to the control group. However, those in the "issues" treatment show significantly *lower* distress at this prospect (p = 0.07); in other words, thinking of partisans in explicitly *non-*identity-based terms seems to depress one's preference for social distance. Meanwhile, subjects in the "traits" condition appear more likely to deem it appropriate to block or defriend someone based on politics, although the difference from the control falls short of statistical significance (p = 0.27).

Taken together, these results suggest that thinking of average partisans in different ways – that is, in terms of traits, political issues, or other social groups – matters for various forms of polarization. Those prompted to think of partisanship as a social identity with its own set of individual-level traits tend to be more affectively and ideologically polarized, and to prefer greater interparty social distance, compared to those who think of party supporters in other ways. Results for perceived ideological polarization prove less conclusive; contra expectations, group- rather than trait-based thinking seems to lead subjects to believe the parties to be more polarized in these terms.

4.5.3 Study 2 Results

While Study 1 brought us a step closer to understanding the relationship between partisan stereotypes and polarization, it suffers from a number of shortcomings. That it is a convenience sample means we cannot generalize these results to the US population as a whole. The size of the sample also poses limitations. The small number of respondents assigned to each treatment condition reduces statistical power, increasing the likelihood of a Type II error; it is possible that real treatment effects went undetected as a result. Further, the design of Study 1 did not allow us to rigorously consider different reactions by respondents' partisanship, which may serve as a moderator. Democrats and Republicans may respond differently to emphasizing different partisan stereotypes, particularly in light of research suggesting that members of the two parties tend to conceive of partisanship itself in distinct ways (Grossmann & Hopkins, 2016). To address these issues, we turn now to our second study on a nationally representative probability sample of 2,015 American adults, block-randomized to account for respondents' partisanship.

Before assessing the impact of the treatments on our outcome variables, we first consider evidence that subjects complied with the study's instructions and that our treatments functioned as intended. These results were discussed in Section 3, but we review them here to emphasize their support for the experimental design. Recall that the treatment had two components – an open-ended response and a checklist task. On both parts, we see indications that subjects took the treatments seriously; the large majority provided responses (about 85 percent to the open-ended tasks and 96 percent to the checklist tasks), and few people seem to have entered a nonsensical response (e.g., checking every box in the checklist task or entering only one word in the open-ended question). With regard to the substance of respondents' reactions to the treatments, we again see evidence that people are responding as intended.

Confident that the bulk of respondents approached the stereotyping tasks as they were meant to, we present the effects of our treatments on affective and ideological dimensions of partisan polarization. Given the directional nature of our hypotheses, significance tests are one-tailed. (In online Appendix B, we additionally present a nonparametric combination (NPC) analysis, which allows us to test the effects of our treatments on all our interrelated outcome variables simultaneously – see Caughey, Dafoe, & Seawright, 2017 – and yields the same results.)

Figure 13 depicts treatment effects on affective polarization (i.e., feeling thermometer difference between the two parties) in the left panel and ideological polarization (i.e., respondents' ideological extremity as measured with

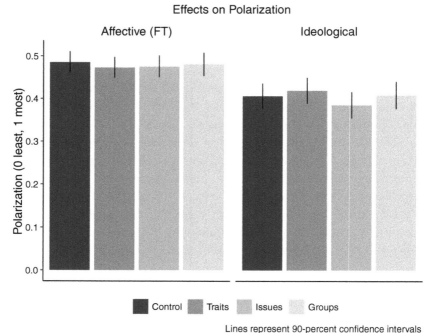

Figure 13 Treatment effects on polarization (TESS sample)

a folded seven-point ideology scale) in the right panel. The treatments show little to no effect when it comes to affective polarization; respondents in all four conditions provide feeling thermometer differentials that are not statistically distinguishable from each other. We do, however, discover notable effects on respondents' own level of ideological polarization; those in the issues condition appear slightly less ideologically extreme than those in the control, but this effect is not statistically significant. More noteworthy, those in the traits condition become more ideologically polarized than those in the issues condition, though the treatment effect falls just short of traditional significance ($p = 0.06$). Thinking of ordinary partisans' issue priorities, rather than their personal traits, appears to reduce ideological extremity.

A closer look at this effect reveals some interesting patterns by respondent partisanship (not shown in the figure; see online Appendix B for details). In the traits condition, relative to the issues condition, Democrats become more ideologically polarized ($p = 0.058$) – as do independents at a lower level of significance ($p = 0.097$) – but Republicans do not. At the same time, Democrats in the groups condition, relative to the control condition, express greater ideological polarization with a greater effect size and a higher degree of significance (p = 0.015) than traits. Given Democrats' propensity to conceive of the parties in terms of their constitutive groups (Grossmann & Hopkins, 2016), it comes as no great surprise if being prompted to think of themselves and their opponents in these terms causes them to polarize.

Moreover, different forms of stereotypic thinking affect the polarization that respondents perceive in the wider political world, as shown in Figure 14. Those asked to consider partisans in terms of their issue priorities, relative to those told to think of traits or groups, perceive rank-and-file *and* congressional partisans as less ideologically distant from each other (and, in the latter case, this proves true for those in the issues condition relative to the control condition as well). Those prompted to think of party supporters' traits perceive a greater ideological divide at the mass level than do those in the control group, in line with our observational findings. This is especially striking, considering that divergent issue priorities, to a large extent, make up the *content* of partisan ideological conflict.

Stereotypes also influence one's preference for social distance from out-partisans. As depicted in Figure 15, relative to the traits, groups, and control

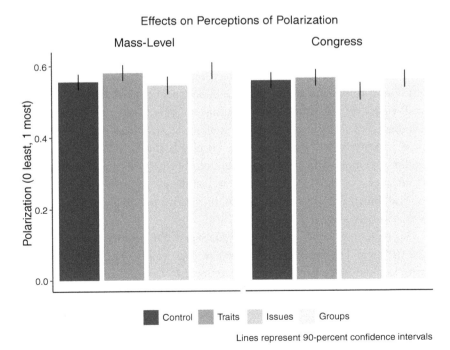

Figure 14 Treatment effects on perceptions of ideological polarization (TESS sample)

Effects on Social Distance and Partisan ID

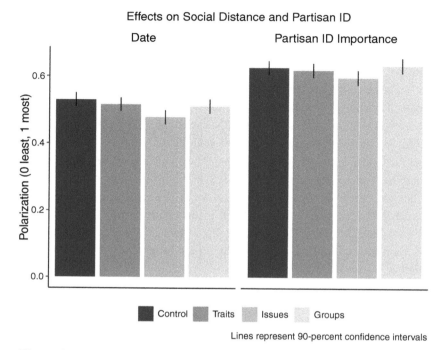

Figure 15 Treatment effects on partisan social distance and partisan identity
(TESS sample)

conditions, subjects in the issues condition express significantly less discomfort at the notion of a family member dating a supporter of the opposing party. The same figure shows similar effects on the importance attached to partisan identity itself – those prompted to think of partisans in terms of issue priorities, relative to those asked to focus on groups or nothing in particular, rate their partisan social identity as less important. (We observe a similar effect for the issues condition compared to the traits condition, but only at a marginal level of significance, $p = 0.081$).[27] In sum, if we ask people to focus on the explicitly political dimension of partisan conflict, they prove less likely to be influenced by partisan divisions in their everyday lives.

This pattern of results supports the findings from our observational data as well as Study 1. Given that trait-based partisan stereotypes most commonly come to mind when people are not prompted to consider specific kinds (see Table 10), it makes sense that respondents in the control group and the traits group display similar levels of polarization. The question, then, becomes how to reorient people's thinking and break this default pattern in order to reduce

---

[27] The effects on partisan social identity appear largely driven by Democratic respondents; see online Appendix B.

partisan conflict. We see decreased levels of affective and ideological polarization when respondents' stereotypes emphasize political issues. This suggests one way to decrease the partisan polarization that permeates the current political environment, a point to which we turn in Section 5.

4.6 Conclusions

After reviewing the results of five data collections – three observational, two experimental – we broadly conclude that partisan stereotype content is politically consequential. The ways that people think about ordinary, mass-level Democrats and Republicans have significant effects on partisan polarization. The question that naturally follows from these results is *why* partisan stereotypes have these effects and the psychological mechanisms behind our findings. We argue that, at least in part, the heightened polarization associated with trait-based stereotypes reflects the social-psychological tendencies resulting from group membership. Conceiving of partisanship as an important social identity of its own, rather than a more straightforwardly instrumental means to political ends, likely prompts an ingroup/outgroup orientation and all the ingroup-enhancement and outgroup-distancing that this entails.

At the same time, we find that a focus on political issues may be depolarizing. Asking people to consider others in terms of the issues they find important, and their beliefs regarding those issues, requires them to "step into their shoes" in a way that asking them to describe those same others in terms of traits or group memberships might not. Prior work in social psychology connects this kind of perspective-taking with reductions in prejudice, implicit bias, and intergroup conflict (Galinsky & Moskowitz, 2000; Todd et al., 2011). Even in the realm of politics, where political issues are ostensibly the objects being fought over, a nudge to consider the other side's perspective has the potential to promote greater tolerance and compromise.

What might account for the mixed pattern of results we observe with regard to group-focused stereotypes? Group-focused stereotypes on the one hand may prime various identities (like religion, class, and race) that could then go on to exacerbate partisan conflict, but on the other hand may emphasize the fact that people belong to some, but not all, of the groups connected to the parties. For people whose other social identities closely align with their partisan affiliation, prompting group-focused stereotypes ought to increase polarization (e.g., Mason, 2016, 2018). For others whose social identities may not be in close accord with their partisanship, stimulating group-focused stereotypes may instead cross-pressure them, awakening feelings of ambivalence toward politics

(Mutz, 2002). Additional work is necessary to assess how people's own collections of group memberships may moderate the relationship between group-focused partisan stereotypes and polarization.

In addition to providing strong support for our arguments, these results also suggest opportunities for future work to address several limitations. Most notably, our research thus far lacks any element of over-time considerations. Given the way that partisan polarization in the United States has developed over time, it seems vital to both (a) document partisan stereotype content at multiple points in time and (b) assess the ways in which partisan stereotypes relate to polarization and other political outcomes at these various points.

Our findings suggest that different kinds of partisan stereotypes influence people's perceptions of the parties and also may induce different levels of affective, ideological, and social polarization. Do these results carry over into the political world, beyond the realm of survey responses? How does partisan stereotyping impact real-world political interactions? Finally, while focusing on political issues may somewhat diminish partisan polarization, are there other stereotype-related interventions that may do so more effectively? Some recent research suggests that counter-stereotypic representations of partisans may lead to increased willingness to socially engage across party lines (Shafranek, 2021) – would instructing people to think counter-stereotypically about partisans have similar effects on affective polarization?

Just as voters' views of the "parties as organizations" and the "parties in government" can be consequential, our work shows that people's ideas about the "party in the electorate" also have meaningful effects on politics. People's stereotypes of ordinary Democrats and Republicans influence not only their perceptions of ideological conflict between the parties, but also their own levels of affective polarization, ideological extremity, and even preferred social distance from members of the other party. Depending on precisely what comes to mind, these stereotypes may ameliorate or exacerbate American political divides. In the next section, we discuss the potential for issue-based stereotypes to reduce partisan conflict and promote a more positive version of party affiliation, which we refer to as responsible partisanship.

5 Responsible Partisanship

In the United States, laments about partisan conflict and polarization have become so numerous that they are almost passé. This is true for both left- and right-leaning outlets; articles titled "America's Political Divides Run Deeper Than Just Republicans And Democrats" and "Partisan Dysfunction Drives

Demand For New Choice" come from the Huffington Post[28] and Fox News,[29] respectively. Prominent Republican and Democratic leaders also bemoan partisan divides. During the first impeachment proceedings for President Trump in 2020, Senator Mitch McConnell decried the articles of impeachment as "a transparently partisan performance from beginning to end".[30] From the other side of the aisle, Senator Richard Durbin said, "Partisan politics must not be our guiding principle throughout this process."[31] In 2020, 91 percent of Americans rated the conflict between Republicans and Democrats as strong or very strong, dwarfing the ratings of strong or very strong conflict between the rich and the poor (59 percent), black and white people (53 percent), the young and old (41 percent), and cities and rural areas (40 percent) (Schaeffer, 2020). There seems to be widespread concern about divisions between Republicans and Democrats and the challenge this divide poses for American government, democracy, and society more generally.

At the same time, large majorities of Americans want their side to win nearly as much as they dislike polarization. One poll reported that while 90 percent of Americans are frustrated by partisan conflict, 80 percent are fed up with political leaders compromising on their values and want politicians who stand up to "the other side" (Balz, 2019). Most people are broadly supportive of the idea of compromise between partisans; however, what they mean by compromise is capitulation from their opponents (Harbridge, Malhotra, & Harrison, 2014).

What, then, are solutions to this state of affairs? When partisans are divided and also deeply committed to their respective sides, what can be done to reduce polarization and conflict? In this Element, we have turned to an examination of Americans' mental images of partisans – their partisan stereotypes – for answers. We first documented how people think of ordinary partisans in the current political climate and then evaluated how different kinds of stereotypes promote or discourage partisan conflict.

We identified three major veins in stereotypes about partisans. Each of these, we have argued, corresponds to a distinct mode of thinking about party affiliation, its functions in the political world, and the scope of its role in an individual's social life. Our studies found: (1) stereotypes focused on *traits*, which we associate with a partisan-identity perspective on partisanship; (2)

[28] www.huffpost.com/entry/republicans-democrats-divided-pew-research_n_59efb2dce4b0b7e63265af9a.
[29] www.foxnews.com/politics/partisan-dysfunction-drives-demand-for-new-choice.
[30] www.republicanleader.senate.gov/newsroom/remarks/mcconnell-on-impeachment-the-transparently-partisan-house-process-is-over-the-senates-time-is-at-hand.
[31] www.nytimes.com/interactive/2019/12/20/us/politics/senators-impeachment-reactions.html.

stereotypes centered on *groups*, associated with a coalitional view of partisanship; and (3) stereotypes mainly about *issue priorities*, which imply a more instrumental view of party affiliation. Trait- or identity-based thinking – which claims the largest share of partisan stereotypes in our survey data – relates to greater polarization in both affective and ideological terms, as well as the perception that the parties in government and in the electorate are further apart ideologically. This connection aligns with past research, which singles out partisan social identity as a root cause of intensified partisan conflict (Iyengar et al., 2019; Mason, 2018). Less common but still prevalent, issue-based thinking about the parties predicts substantial reductions in polarization on all of these same dimensions.

What are the practical implications of these findings? How might the depolarizing effects of issue-based stereotypes be harnessed to de-escalate partisan conflict? We take up that question in this final section. First, we review other interventions suggested by the extant academic literature for reducing partisan conflict, identifying their potential benefits and limitations. Drawing upon these past insights and our own findings, we ultimately advocate for a version of *responsible partisanship* that emphasizes policy as the foundation of differences between the parties, rather than group memberships or fundamental traits. Such an approach, we believe, can help to mitigate conflict and polarization between Republicans and Democrats in the United States.

5.1 Interventions Suggested by Past Research

Recent political science scholarship has investigated what kinds of interventions might diminish the partisan divide. Below, we outline potential causes of polarization – as well as potential solutions – found in such work. While each stream of research we discuss has contributed a piece to the puzzle, we contend that the findings in this Element provide an important, novel explanation for partisan conflict in the United States. We argue, as well, that the fixes suggested by these other studies, though insightful and valuable, suffer from some shortcomings and pitfalls. Following this discussion, we offer our own recommendations for mitigating polarization based on our findings, and we explain why we consider them more practical and realistic than the avenues presented in other works.

5.1.1 Elite Signals

Much of the current era's polarization can be laid at the feet of political elites. Though debate continues as to just how ideologically polarized the mass public is, partisans in government have become substantially more divided in recent decades (Hetherington, 2009). This development has not gone unnoticed among the mass public, with ordinary citizens increasingly likely to perceive significant differences between the parties (Hetherington, 2001; Levendusky, 2009), and they may shift or solidify their partisan allegiances and issue attitudes as a result (Carsey & Layman, 2006; Layman & Carsey, 2002). This kind of cue-taking leads to greater consistency among voters (Levendusky, 2010), which is generally considered a normative good. However, elite polarization and signaling are also likely to deepen political and social conflict among rank-and-file partisans.

The flip side of this dynamic, though, is that perceptions of elites and their views may also depolarize the electorate under the right circumstances. When partisans in Congress, for example, appear divided on an issue, mass partisans tend to adjust their opinions accordingly – and, notably, without regard for the strength of arguments for different sides of that issue (Druckman, Peterson, & Slothuus, 2013; also see Mullinix, 2016). Conversely, when congressional partisans are presented as *not* polarized, the merits of different policy arguments take precedence over partisan loyalty (Druckman, Peterson, & Slothuus, 2013). Elite cues may thus produce more deliberative, less tribal citizens.

Nonetheless, this avenue for reducing polarization strikes us as limited for a number of reasons. First, while non-polarized cues may moderate attitude extremity around a specific issue debate, it remains unclear whether these effects would carry over to mass partisans' overall ideological extremity. Second, as we have emphasized at various points, affective polarization occurs even in the absence of substantive political disagreement (Iyengar et al., 2019; Mason, 2018) – so seeing party elites as less divided on the issues may do little to curb feelings of general partisan hostility. Finally, while it may be easy enough to portray the parties as non-polarized in the context of an experiment, in the real world they seem only to be growing further apart, with plenty of media coverage to make this clear to citizens (Levendusky & Malhotra, 2016b; Prior, 2013; Robison & Mullinix, 2016). In such an environment, to convince most Americans that the parties in government are *not* polarized seems a monumental ask. Further, given the reality that Republican and Democratic elites and party activists are increasingly divided from one another (McCarty, Poole, & Rosenthal, 2016), this kind of messaging may cross over from well-intentioned to manipulative and deceptive.

5.1.2 Mass-Level Misperceptions and Corrections

Another large share of interparty hostility seems to stem from misperceptions about the other side, especially at the mass level. Members of both parties tend to see Democrats and Republicans, as well as liberals and conservatives, as further apart in terms of ideology and policy than they are in reality (Ahler, 2014; Levendusky & Malhotra, 2016a). Media portrayals of partisan conflict likely exacerbate these mistaken beliefs, often framing partisan conflict as a battle over fundamental values (Levendusky & Malhotra, 2016b; Prior, 2013; Robison & Mullinix, 2016). Such overestimates of ideological polarization may then prove self-fulfilling, driving partisans to adopt views that mirror the extremity they perceive (Ahler, 2014). Along related lines, perceptions that partisans diverge in terms of their personal and social values predict more negative affect toward the opposing party and less willingness to engage in political action alongside outpartisans (Howat, 2019). Thus, the media environment, exaggerated perceptions of partisan conflict, and reactions to those perceptions create a kind of polarization feedback loop.

The influence of misperceptions goes beyond explicitly political considerations. People often overestimate the proportions of partisans, especially outpartisans, who belong to party-stereotypic groups. For example, they estimate the percentage of Democrats who identify as LGBT at 32 percent (compared to 6 percent in reality) and the percentage of Republicans who make over $250,000 per year at 38 percent (2 percent in actuality) – exaggerations by factors of more than five and almost twenty, respectively (Ahler & Sood, 2018). Similar misperceptions significantly overestimate the proportion of evangelicals among Republicans and the non-religious among Democrats, a divide especially likely to exacerbate the "culture war" (Claassen et al., 2021). Misperceptions about the groups that make up the parties are likely to incite greater affective polarization, belief in greater ideological distance between the parties, and stronger adherence to one's own partisan identity (Ahler & Sood, 2018; Claassen et al., 2021). Feelings about the parties' constitutive groups bear strongly on attitudes about the parties themselves (Robison & Moskowitz, 2019), so if people exaggerate the "otherness" of the opposing party's coalition, it comes as no surprise that partisan conflict should intensify.

Interparty misperceptions may be corrected, however, with respect to both ideological and coalitional dimensions. People who are informed of the actual policy positions held by typical liberals and conservatives tend to adopt significantly more moderate views (Ahler, 2014). Those provided with the parties' actual demographic compositions, meanwhile, come to see opposing party supporters as less extreme and express less desire for social distance from outpartisans (Ahler & Sood, 2018). Contact with counter-stereotypic outpartisans shows a similar effect on the desire for interpary social distance, even in a domain as personal as roommate choice (Shafranek, 2021). These studies demonstrate, first, that at least some partisans remain open to having their images of partisans corrected and, second, that they may depolarize as a result.

Corrections, however, are inherently limited by the degree to which perceptions among the public diverge from real differences between partisans. They clearly do, to a considerable degree; however, Democrats and Republicans remain divided in very real ways. Whether one examines ideology and policy attitudes (Abramowitz & Saunders, 2006), divergent group interests (Achen & Bartels, 2016; Hetherington & Weiler, 2009), demographic composition (Pew Research Center, 2020; Mason, 2018), or fundamental worldviews (Goren, 2013; Oliver & Wood, 2018), modern partisan conflict appears far from baseless. Our own data show that the public recognizes many of these divisions. Therefore, corrections concerning the sources of partisan conflict can only go so far, and, in the case of the deepest divisions between partisans, correction may not be possible at all.

5.1.3 Overcoming Partisan Divisions with a Common Identity

Perhaps the strength of some other identity can overcome the divisive effects of partisanship. All people possess multiple social identities, a fact which creates the potential to alter their perceptions of themselves and others by raising the salience of one identity while downplaying the rest (Gaertner & Dovidio, 2000; Kang & Bodenhausen, 2015). The Common Ingroup Identity Model (CIIM; Gaertner & Dovidio, 2000; Gaertner et al., 1989) suggests that members of groups in conflict may be prompted to recategorize themselves into a well-liked, superordinate identity to which both groups belong. Doing so has the potential to reduce intergroup antipathy.

Levendusky (2018) applies these insights to affective polarization by emphasizing American national identity over partisan identity in a series of survey experiments. Such an identity, in broad terms, consists of "a subjective or internalized sense of belonging to the nation" (Huddy & Khatib, 2007, 65), and this feeling of national attachment goes beyond racial and partisan boundaries (Citrin, Wong, & Duff, 2001; Huddy & Khatib, 2007; Theiss-Morse, 2009). If people can be persuaded to think of themselves – and their political opponents – as Americans rather than partisans, polarization may diminish. This appears to be the case; partisans primed with American identity exhibit significantly higher affective ratings of the opposing party and, in the case of Republican respondents, of President Obama (Levendusky, 2018). These effects manifest even among strong partisans, and they are not confined to an experimental context – observational survey data suggest that a spike in patriotism around July 4, 2008 similarly raised affective evaluations of the opposing party (Levendusky, 2018). Even fervent party supporters can be induced to think of themselves as Americans first and partisans second.

This strategy, too, suffers from limitations. Levendusky (2018) acknowledges that politicians – being partisan figures themselves – may be unable to appeal to American identity in an effective way, as observers are likely to filter these and other cues through a partisan lens (also see Nicholson, 2012). Other work, moreover, suggests that this approach may have other shortcomings – even dangers. While there is a good deal of agreement among the public concerning the content and boundaries of American identity, the consensus is far from absolute. Most notably for present purposes, partisan divisions exist with respect to which characteristics are seen as important to being American (e.g., speaking English, believing in God, diversity and assimilation; Theiss-Morse, 2009; Schildkraut, 2014). Attempts to reduce partisan conflict by centering American identity may thus lead to conflict over what it precisely means to be American, or perhaps shift the conflict from partisanship to other divisions such as ethnicity or religion. Indeed, political scientists have long noticed a darker side to increases in national identity and patriotism, which may promote exclusionary attitudes (Sniderman, Hagendoorn, & Prior, 2004; Wong, 2010) and even diminish support for democratic norms and rights (Parker, 2010). Such concerns seem especially relevant in the United States' current political climate.

More broadly, a common ingroup identity has the potential to *increase* rather than decrease partisan conflict. For a superordinate identity to promote intergroup harmony or cooperation, members of that identity's constitutive groups must define the identity in similar terms (Brewer, 1999). If they do not, the CIIM will not only fail to reduce conflict but also exacerbate intergroup biases (for example, under conditions that make gender salient to politics, Democratic women become less trusting of Republican women, and vice versa; see Klar, 2018). Priming a common identity for partisans thus may hurt more than it helps.

5.2 Our Proposed Alternative: Promoting "Responsible Partisanship"

What sort of interventions might serve to attenuate polarization in a more pragmatic, reliable way? We believe the findings presented in this Element, combined with insights from past work, provide an answer. Partisanship will not cease to be a central dimension of American political conflict any time soon. As an enormous body of research and the foregoing sections indicate, partisan concerns permeate elections, policymaking, the media landscape, and everyday social life. These facts seem unlikely to change and may ultimately be *impossible* to change. Vigorous debate and conflict are necessary to democracy and, as E. E. Schattschneider famously asserted, "modern democracy is unthinkable save in terms of the parties" (1942, 1). Parties give order and coherence to political conflicts that might otherwise result in chaos, which the public and even the politicians themselves could not comprehend or manage (Aldrich, 2011). The nature of politics, combined with the particulars of the American electoral system,[32] virtually guarantees that bipolar partisan conflict is here to stay.

What might change, however, is the way in which most Americans *engage with* the conflict. For insights into this possibility, and how the public's thinking around partisanship might be reoriented, we draw upon the classic "responsible parties" thesis put forth in a well-known report by the American Political Science Association's Committee on Political Parties. Responsible parties, in brief, present distinct policy alternatives to the electorate and commit to those policies (APSA, 1950). In this (admittedly idealized) paradigm, voters are provided with a sufficiently diverse range of policies to choose from – and, should they prove dissatisfied with one party's performance in government, to reject. Responsible parties, in other words, help to organize political debate, facilitate informed electoral choices, and produce meaningful electoral outcomes.

Of course, the APSA report observed in 1950 that the two major parties, as organizations, were *not* adequately fulfilling these democratic functions. This state of affairs has improved in some ways since then; voters have come to perceive clearer differences between the parties (Hetherington, 2001), and this development has in turn made many voters more consistent in their political attitudes (Levendusky, 2010). Some work even suggests that more polarized elected officials actually provide better representation of their constituents' interests (Ahler & Broockman, 2018). On the whole, however, "The defining characteristic of our moment is that parties are weak while partisanship is strong" (Azari, 2016), and a growing number of partisans no longer view their political opponents as legitimate. As Schlozman and Rosenfeld (2019) observe, we need look no further than the 2016 election, the way it surprised so many pundits and scholars, and myriad developments in partisan politics since then to see these effects in action. Clear examples also occurred around the 2020 presidential election; the refusal of many prominent Republican figures (Donald Trump most notably among them) to accept the legitimacy of President Biden's

---

[32] That is to say, single-member districts and plurality elections, which, according to Duverger's law and other theories, create strong pressures toward a two-party system (Duverger, 1963, 217–28; Schattschneider, 1942, 69).

victory (Collinson, 2021), support for conspiratorial demonization of outpartisans through movements like QAnon (Roose, 2020), and the violent targeting of elected officials during the pro-Trump insurrection at the US Capitol (Hoskin, 2021) all suggest that partisan divisions are getting deeper, sharper, and more dangerous.

At the same time the political waters have become ideologically clearer, the rise in affective polarization (Iyengar et al., 2019) and negative partisanship (Abramowitz & Webster, 2016; Bankert, 2020) has muddied them in other ways. Partisanship, as we have discussed, has become personalized and essentialized among the electorate, with Democratic and Republican supporters expressing a deep dislike of each other not because of policy disagreement, but simply because they identify with opposing sides. This approach to partisanship undermines the benefits of more "responsible parties" as citizens no longer hold parties accountable for their positions or performance. This tendency weakens the incentives for parties to promote clear agendas and live up to their promises. As an antidote to this harmful pattern, whereas the APSA committee advocated for responsible parties at the organizational level, we make a similar recommendation at the mass level: the promotion of *responsible partisanship*. By this, we mean a mode of thinking in which partisans view each other not as fundamentally different kinds of people with irreconcilable differences, but as distinct groups of citizens whose disparate policy priorities can be productively debated and compromised on.[33]

We are not the first researchers to draw links between the APSA report and the behavior of mass-level partisans (see Pomper & Weiner, 2002; Weisberg, 2002),[34] but we believe our work is uniquely suited to demonstrate what responsible partisanship in the electorate might look like. Recall our key findings. First, *trait*-based stereotypes are the most common variety of mass-level partisan stereotypes, comprising a plurality if not a majority of the mental images reported by our survey respondents. Holding such stereotypes predicts greater individual-level affective polarization and ideological extremity, as well as perceptions of more intense ideological polarization between the parties at the mass and elite levels. Our second study found, however, that people prompted to think of ordinary partisans in terms of their *issue* priorities display less polarization on the same dimensions. Thus, if the parties in the electorate could be persuaded to think of each other in these terms – rather than as tribes of people fundamentally different in their personal characteristics and beliefs – the shape of partisan conflict could change.

---

[33] We are not, however, the first to coin the term responsible partisanship. In particular, we take note of a book of the same name edited by Green and Herrnson (2003).

[34] And, as these authors note, parties in the electorate were virtually absent from the original report.

Unlike some approaches to reducing polarization, our recommendation does not require downplaying the prevalence or depth of partisan conflict. This is fortunate, given the extent to which ordinary citizens take their cues from partisan elites (Druckman, Peterson, & Slothuus, 2013; Hetherington, 2001; Levendusky, 2010) and the fact that those elites have increasingly polarized in recent decades (Hetherington, 2009; Lee, 2009; McCarty, Poole, & Rosenthal, 2016) – both factors which make it difficult to convince people that the parties are less divided than they are. Even if we could do so, as mentioned, that kind of deception strikes us as ethically questionable. So, instead, we advocate efforts to change what people think this conflict is primarily *about*.

Some readers may look at this recommendation and conclude that we are arguing against "identity politics" and encouraging members of the public to disregard the relationship of parties and politics to social groups in American society. This is not what we are suggesting. We hope, on the contrary, our earlier discussion makes clear that we believe group-based conflict is not only inevitable but also *healthy* for democratic politics. Political parties exist, from one perspective, as amalgamations of groups based on class, race, gender, and other identities (e.g., Campbell et al., 1960; Achen & Bartels, 2016), and our own findings suggest that the American public is well aware of this fact. These divisions are not, in and of themselves, the problem in our view. Different groups of people will always have and express particularistic interests and demands, which a democratic system must seek to address and balance. Thus, we do not caution against identity politics, but against *essentialized* politics in which groups – parties included – are treated as divided due to unchangeable, intrinsic differences. Now, with this important caveat out of the way, let us proceed to our concrete recommendations.

5.3 Ways to Foster Responsible Partisanship

Concerning prospects for promoting responsible partisanship in the electorate, our findings give cause for optimism. Descriptive results from the studies presented in this Element indicate broad, pre-existing public awareness of issue-based conflict between the parties. When people's top-of-the-head partisan images concern political issues, they generally assign the correct positions and priorities to each party. Political interest moderates this tendency some-what, but respondents at all levels of political engagement correctly identify the parties' key issues more often than not. And while this may not be convincing evidence of deep political sophistication, it does suggest that, on average, people have the knowledge needed to focus on issue-based differences. Most notably, respondents in our experimental study's "issues" condition, who were asked specifically to think about rank-and-file partisans' issue priorities, show a strong trend toward depolarization, despite their recognition of many partisan issue divisions.

Such an intervention seems both feasible and likely to have a real impact – not just in an experimental context but in the real political world. Past research, particularly on misperceptions (Ahler, 2014; Ahler & Sood, 2018; Levendusky & Malhotra, 2016a), suggests that images of the parties and their supporters are mutable and that efforts to change them may dampen polarization. Our approach should be even more effective and applicable to different contexts, in that we are not limited only to correcting inaccurate beliefs about outpartisans (a correction that is constrained by the amount of incorrect information some-one initially believes). Instead, we propose mainly to remind people of what many of them already know about issue-based disagreements between the parties. Rather than attempting to correct or otherwise alter people's percep-tions, we suggest priming them to increase the salience of issue-based divisions (correspondingly decreasing the salience of other dimensions that we have shown to be associated with heightened polarization).

Just as the classic notion of responsible parties requires partisan elites to send clear, sincere signals about their policy priorities to the electorate, our vision of responsible *partisanship* asks ordinary partisans to (1) articulate sincerely their own political views and (2) make honest efforts to learn and understand their opponents' positions. This dynamic, we believe, explains why an issue-based focus, relative to a traits- or groups-based focus, would diminish polarization in the ways we have observed. We discussed briefly in Section 4 that thinking about partisans' issue priorities, compared to other forms of stereotypic think-ing, likely involves a degree of perspective-taking – that is, active consideration of alternative viewpoints or others' psychological experiences. Perspective-taking has the potential to improve relations between groups in myriad ways (Todd & Galinsky, 2014). To our knowledge, its impact has not been examined in depth with respect to interparty conflict; however, in areas such as racial bias, perspective-taking may improve evaluations of outgroup members (Todd et al., 2011), prevent the application of group-based stereotypes (Galinsky & Moskowitz, 2000), and even reduce the maintenance of such stereotypes in memory (Todd, Galinsky, & Bodenhausen, 2012). The benefits extend beyond intergroup attitudes, as well – perspective-takers display more positive behav-iors in interactions with outgroup members, who are themselves more likely to perceive those interactions favorably (Todd et al., 2011). These findings align with research in political science concerning exposure to partisan disagreement within social networks; people exposed to the viewpoints of opposing partisans prove less likely to place importance on their partisan identities (Robison, 2020;

c.f., Levendusky, Druckman, & McLain, 2016), a commonly recognized source of affective and other polarization (e.g., Iyengar, Sood, & Lelkes, 2012). The kind of interparty perspective-taking that our results imply could go a long way toward improving social, if not political, relations between party supporters.

This kind of responsible partisanship, rooted in real issue-based differences, might be promoted among the electorate in a number of ways. Perhaps most straightforwardly, the news media could play a large part in fostering more responsible forms of partisan thinking. It is, after all, the media's traditional role to inform the public about the key political debates of the day, which includes policy divisions between the parties. News outlets, as well as organizations like Gallup and the Pew Research Center, already provide coverage of policy-based conflicts as well as public opinion on the issues. At the same time, however, current styles of media reporting may be partly responsible for exaggerated perceptions of the conflict between the parties (Levendusky & Malhotra, 2016b). Media coverage of partisan debates, as mentioned, often portray Democrats and Republicans as divided by fundamental values (Robison & Mullinix, 2016), and while there is certainly truth to this claim (Goren, 2013), drawing too much attention to these underlying conflicts may harm prospects for interparty dialogue and compromise. And, of course, the media are often accused of focusing too much on process, "horse race" coverage of campaigns, and so on, rather than the substance of the issues. We find ourselves, then, asking for the same changes to news reporting that democratic theorists have been demanding for decades, if not centuries.

We might instead turn to political elites themselves, who have shaped and will continue to shape the public's impressions of partisan conflict (Hetherington, 2001; Levendusky, 2010; Zaller, 1992). To do so would put us in a similar position to that of the 1950 APSA committee: advocating that party organizations and elites clearly and accurately articulate their policy priorities (as well as their opponents' priorities) and follow through on them when in government. Unfortunately, such a forthright approach does not always constitute a winning strategy in politics, and many politicians benefit considerably from the current polarized climate. Moreover, if party leaders largely did not heed the APSA committee's recommendations seventy years ago, during a time of much less polarization, we are not so naive as to think many of them would take our advice today.

Thus, we expect neither a great upsurge in substantive news reporting, nor a sudden wave of honest, positive campaigning, to promote widespread responsible partisanship. Plausible interventions, at least for the foreseeable future, will have to remain much more targeted in their scope and more marginal in their impact.

Several promising efforts from advocacy groups may promote responsible partisanship. One, Braver Angels, organizes events to bring together people from different sides of the political spectrum to have honest and respectful conversations about their disagreements. These experiences emphasize learning to understand political opponents' points of view and to find common ground.[35] Another organization, OpenMind, trains individuals to develop empathy and understanding for others, including across partisan differences.[36] These efforts tap into many of the same principles we have discussed here and would go a long way to promote more responsible partisanship in the American public. We would encourage the creation of more groups like these, as well as opportunities for these organizations to implement their programs and events on a larger scale. Rigorous research can accompany these efforts to evaluate which techniques promote responsible partisanship and which do not. Such research, and the organizations themselves, might receive funding from government and various private foundations, all of which would likely benefit from improving political and social relations between the parties.

Whatever the tactic, members of the American public need encouragement and motivation to develop more responsible partisanship. As our research shows, tribal, trait-based thinking is common and can be the default way of thinking for many people, and such patterns may prove difficult to overcome on one's own. People have the capacity and knowledge to shift their approach to partisanship, but someone or something must push them to do so. Efforts on the part of the media, elites, and organized groups are therefore crucial to changing the tenor of partisan conflict in the United States, and further research and innovations are critical to determine which specific strategies will be most effective. Despite its benefits, responsible partisanship is unlikely to emerge of its own accord; in fact, responses to the current political environment seem to be either increased polarization or heightened disgust and disengagement with politics (Klar, Krupnikov, & Ryan, 2018). Neither of these reactions seems likely to reduce partisan conflict – increasing polarization will exacerbate the problems created by less responsible partisanship, and increasing disengagement will give even more say to polarized individuals and groups.

We are encouraged, rather than deflated, by these findings about the partisan stereotypes held by the American public. With effort, additional research, and a desire to address partisan divides, the nature of political conflict in the United States can change. Whether academics, media, elected officials, and organizations will have the desire to help the public make these changes remains an open question – one that we hope will be answered in the affirmative.

---

[35] For more specifics on the approach of Braver Angels, see https://braverangels.org/.
[36] More details can be found at https://openmindplatform.org/.

References

Abrajano, M. & Hajnal, Z. L. (2017). *White Backlash: Immigration, Race, and American Politics*. Princeton, NJ: Princeton University Press.

Abramowitz, A. I. & Saunders, K. L. (2006). Exploring the Bases of Partisanship in the American Electorate: Social Identity vs. Ideology. *Political Research Quarterly*, 59(2), 175–87.

Abramowitz, A. I. & Saunders, K. L. (2008). Is Polarization a Myth? *Journal of Politics*, 70(2), 542–55.

Abramowitz, A. I. & Webster, S. (2016). The Rise of Negative Partisanship and the Nationalization of Elections in the 21st Century. *Electoral Studies*, 41, 12–22.

Abrams, D. & Hogg, M. A. (1988). Comments on the Motivational Status of Self-Esteem in Social Identity and Intergroup Discrimination. *European Journal of Social Psychology*, 18(4), 317–34.

Achen, C. H. & Bartels, L. M. (2016). *Democracy for Realists: Why Elections Do Not Produce Responsive Government*. Princeton, NJ: Princeton University Press.

Ahler, D. J. (2014). Self-Fulfilling Misperceptions of Public Polarization. *Journal of Politics*, 76(3), 607–20.

Ahler, D. J. & Broockman, D. E. (2018). The Delegate Paradox: Why Polarized Politicians Can Represent Citizens Best. *Journal of Politics*, 80 (4), 1117–33.

Ahler, D. J. & Sood, G. (2018). The Parties in Our Heads: Misperceptions about Party Composition and Their Consequences. *Journal of Politics*, 80(3), 964–81.

Aldrich, J. H. (2011). *Why Parties? A Second Look*. Chicago, IL: University of Chicago Press.

Allport, G. W. (1954). *The Nature of Prejudice*. Reading, MA: Addison-Wesley.

American Political Science Association (APSA) (1950). Summary of Conclusions and Proposals. *American Political Science Review*, 44(3, Part 2, Supplement), 1–14.

Appel, M., Weber, S., & Kronberger, N. (2015). The Influence of Stereotype Threat on Immigrants: Review and Meta-Analysis. *Frontiers in Psychology*, 6. https://doi.org/10.3389/fpsyg.2015.00900.

Ashmore, R. D. & Del Boca, F. K. (1981). Conceptual Approaches to Stereotypes and Stereotyping. In D. L. Hamilton, ed., *Cognitive Processes in Stereotyping and Intergroup Behavior*. Hillsdale, NJ: Lawrence Erlbaum Associates.

Azari, J. (2016). Weak Parties and Strong Partisanship are a Bad Combination. Vox, November 3. www.vox.com/mischiefs-of-faction/2016/11/3/13512362/weak-parties-strong-partisanship-bad-combination.

Ballard, J. (2019). Fewer Than Half of Americans are Comfortable Dating Someone From the Opposite Political Party. YouGov, October 24. https://today.yougov.com/topics/relationships/articles-reports/2019/10/24/politics-beliefs-friends-partners-poll-survey.

Balz, D. (2019). Americans Hate All the Partisanship, But They're Also More Partisan Than They Were. *The Washington Post*, October 26. www.washingtonpost.com/politics/americans-hate-all-the-partisanship-but-theyre-also-more-partisan-than-they-were/2019/10/26/e1f4abe2-f762-11e9-a285-882a8e386a96_story.html.

Banda, K. K. & Cluverius, J. (2018). Elite Polarization, Party Extremity, and Affective Polarization. *Electoral Studies*, 56, 90–101.

Bankert, A. (2020). Negative and Positive Partisanship in the 2016 U.S. Presidential Election. *Political Behavior*. https://doi.org/10.1007/s11109-020-09599-1.

Bargh, J. A., Chen, M., & Burrows, L. (1996). Automaticity of Social Behavior: Direct Effects of Trait Construct and Stereotype Activation on Action. *Journal of Personality and Social Psychology*, 7(2), 230–44.

Bauer, N. M. (2019). Gender Stereotyping in Political Decision Making. In *Oxford Research Encyclopedia of Politics*. https://doi.org/10.1093/acrefore/9780190228637.013.772.

Bauer, N. M., Yong, L. H., & Krupnikov, Y. (2017). Who is Punished? Conditions Affecting Voter Evaluations of Legislators Who Do Not Compromise. *Political Behavior*, 39(2), 279–300.

Baumer, D. C. & Gold, H. J. (1995). Party Images and the American Electorate. *American Politics Quarterly*, 23(1), 33–61.

Baumer, D. C. & Gold, H. J. (2007). Party Images and Partisan Resurgence. *The Social Science Journal*, 44(3), 465–79.

Berelson, B. R., Lazarsfeld, P. F., & McPhee, W. N. (1954). *Voting*. Chicago, IL: University of Chicago Press.

Berinsky, A. J. & Mendelberg, T. (2005). The Indirect Effects of Discredited Stereotypes in Judgments of Jewish Leaders. *American Journal of Political Science*, 49(4), 845–64.

Biernat, M. (2003). Toward a Broader View of Social Stereotyping. *American Psychologist*, 58(12), 1019–27.

Bigler, R. S. & Liben, L. S. (2007). Developmental Intergroup Theory: Explaining and Reducing Children's Social Stereotyping and Prejudice. *Current Directions in Psychological Science*, 16(3), 162–6.

Bodenhausen, G. V. & Lichtenstein, M. (1987). Social Stereotypes and Information-Processing Strategies: The Impact of Task Complexity. *Journal of Personality and Social Psychology*, 52(5), 871–80.

Bodenhausen, G. V. & Wyer, R. S. (1985). Effects of Stereotypes on Decision Making and Information-Processing Strategies. *Journal of Personality and Social Psychology*, 48(2), 267–82.

Bordalo, P., Coffman, K., Gennaioli, N., & Shleifer, A. (2016). Stereotypes. *Quarterly Journal of Economics*, 141(4), 1753–94.

Brader, T., Tucker, J. A., & Therriault, A. (2014). Cross Pressure Scores: An Individual-Level Measure of Cumulative Partisan Pressures Arising from Social Group Memberships. *Political Behavior*, 36(1), 23–51.

Brandt, M. J. & Reyna, C. (2012). The Functions of Symbolic Racism. *Social Justice Research*, 25(1), 41–60.

Brandt, M. J. & Van Tongeren, D. R. (2017). People Both High and Low on Religious Fundamentalism Are Prejudiced Toward Dissimilar Groups. *Journal of Personality and Social Psychology*, 112(1), 76–97.

Brewer, M. B. (1999). The Psychology of Prejudice: Ingroup Love and Outgroup Hate? *Journal of Social Issues*, 55(3), 429–44.

Brewer, M. D. (2009). *Party Images in the American Electorate*. New York: Routledge.

Bullock, J. G. (2011). Elite Influence on Public Opinion in an Informed Electorate. *American Political Science Review*, 105(3), 496–515.

Campbell, A., Converse, P. E., Miller, W. E., & Stokes, D. E. (1960). *The American Voter*. New York: Wiley.

Carmines, E. G. & Stimson, J. A. (1989). *Issue Evolution: Race and the Transformation of American Politics*. Princeton, NJ: Princeton University Press.

Carsey, T. M. & Layman, G. C. (2006). Changing Sides or Changing Minds? Party Identification and Policy Preferences in the American Electorate. *American Journal of Political Science*, 50(2), 464–77.

Cassese, E. C. (2019). Partisan Dehumanization in American Politics. *Political Behavior*. https://doi.org/10.1007/s11109-019-09545-w.

Cassese, E. C. & Holman, M. R. (2018). Party and Gender Stereotypes in Campaign Attacks. *Political Behavior*, 40(3), 785–807.

Caughey, D., Dafoe, A., & Seawright, J. (2017). Nonparametric Combination (NPC): A Framework for Testing Elaborate Theories. *Journal of Politics*, 79(2), 688–701.

Cesario, J., Plaks, J. E., & Higgins, E. T. (2006). Automatic Social Behavior as Motivated Preparation to Interact. *Journal of Personality and Social Psychology*, 90(6), 893–910.

Chambers, J. R., Baron, R. S., & Inman, M. L. (2006). Misperceptions in Intergroup Conflict: Disagreeing About What We Disagree About. *Psychological Science*, 17(1), 38–45.

Chen, M. & Bargh, J. A. (1997). Nonconscious Behavioral Confirmation Processes: The Self-Fulfilling Consequences of Automatic Stereotype Activation. *Journal of Experimental Social Psychology*, 33(5), 541–60.

Citrin, J., Wong, C., & Duff, B. (2001). The Meaning of American National Identity: Patterns of Ethnic Conflict and Consensus. In R. D. Ashmore, L. Jussim, & D. Wilder, eds., *Social Identity, Intergroup Conflict, and Conflict Reduction*. New York: Oxford University Press, pp. 71–100.

Claassen, R. L., Djupe, P. A., Lewis, A. R., & Neiheisel, J. R. (2021). Which Party Represents My Group? The Group Foundations of Partisan Choice and Polarization. *Political Behavior* 43(2): 615–36.

Clifford, S. (2020). Compassionate Democrats and Tough Republicans: How Ideology Shapes Partisan Stereotypes. *Political Behavior*, 42(4), 1269–93.

Collinson, S. (2021). Trump's False Election Fraud Claims Face a Dead End in Congress. CNN, January 6. www.cnn.com/2021/01/06/politics/donald-trump-mike-pence-congress/index.html.

Conover, P. J. & Feldman, S. (1989). Candidate Perception in an Ambiguous World: Campaigns, Cues, and Inference Processes. *American Journal of Political Science*, 33(4), 912–40.

Converse, P. E. (1964). The Nature of Belief Systems in Mass Publics. In D. E. Apter, ed., *Ideology and Its Discontents*. New York: Wiley, pp. 206–61.

Crawford, J. T., Jussim, L., Madon, S., Cain, T. R., & Stevens, S. T. (2011). The Use of Stereotypes and Individuating Information in Political Person Perception. *Personality and Social Psychology Bulletin*, 37(4), 529–42.

Devine, P. G. (1989). Stereotypes and Prejudice: Their Automatic and Controlled Components. *Journal of Personality and Social Psychology*, 56(1), 5–18.

Devine, P. G. & Elliot, A. J. (1995). Are Racial Stereotypes Really Fading? The Princeton Trilogy Revisited. *Personality and Social Psychology Bulletin*, 21 (11), 1139–50.

Dietrich, B. J. (2021). Using Motion Detection to Measure Social Polarization in the U.S. House of Representatives. *Political Analysis*, 29(2), 250–9.

Doyen, S., Klein, O., Pichon, C.-L., & Cleeremans, A. (2012). Behavioral Priming: It's All in the Mind, but Whose Mind? *PLoS ONE*, 7, e29081.

Druckman, J. N. & Kam, C. D. (2011). Students as Experimental Participants: A Defense of the "Narrow Data Base." In J. N. Druckman, D. P. Green, J. H. J. H. Kuklinski, & A. Lupia, eds., *Cambridge Handbook of Experimental Political Science*. New York: Cambridge University Press, pp. 41–57.

Druckman, J. N. & Levendusky, M. S. (2019). What Do We Measure When We Measure Affective Polarization? *Public Opinion Quarterly*, 83(1), 114–22.

Druckman, J. N., Peterson, E., & Rune Slothuus, R. (2013). How Elite Partisan Polarization Affects Public Opinion Formation. *American Political Science Review*, 107(1), 57–79.

Duverger, M. (1963). *Political Parties*. New York: Wiley.

Eagly, A. H. & Mladinic, A. (1989). Gender Stereotypes and Attitudes toward Women and Men. *Personality and Social Psychology Bulletin*, 15(4), 543–58.

Engelhardt, A. M. & Utych, S. M. (2018). Grand Old (Tailgate) Party? Partisan Discrimination in Apolitical Settings. *Political Behavior*, 42(3), 769–89.

Fiorina, M. P. & Abrams, S. J. (2008). Political Polarization in the American Public. *Annual Review of Political Science*, 11, 563–88.

Fiorina, M. P., Abrams, S. J., & Pope, J. C. (2005). *Culture War? The Myth of a Polarized America*. New York: Pearson Longman.

Fiske, S. T., Cuddy, A. J. C., Glick, P., & Xu, J. (2002). A Model of (Often Mixed) Stereotype Content: Competence and Warmth Respectively Follow From Perceived Status and Competition. *Journal of Personality and Social Psychology*, 82(6), 878–902.

Gaertner, S. L. & Dovidio, J. F. (2000). *Reducing Intergroup Bias: The Common Ingroup Identity Model*. Philadelphia, PA: Psychology Press.

Gaertner, S. L., Mann, J., Murrell, A., & Dovidio, J. F. (1989). Reducing Intergroup Bias: The Benefits of Recategorization. *Journal of Personality and Social Psychology*, 57(2), 239–49.

Galinsky, A. D., Hall, E. V., & Cuddy, A. J. C. (2013). Gendered Races: Implications for Interracial Marriage, Leadership Selection, and Athletic Participation. *Psychological Science*, 24(4), 498–506.

Galinsky, A. D. & Moskowitz, G. B. (2000). Perspective-Taking: Decreasing Stereotype Expression, Stereotype Accessibility, and In-Group Favoritism. *Journal of Personality and Social Psychology*, 78(4), 708–24.

Geer, J. G. (1991). The Electorate's Partisan Evaluations: Evidence of a Continuing Democratic Edge. *Public Opinion Quarterly*, 55(2), 218–31.

Gerring, J. (2012). Mere Description. *British Journal of Political Science*, 42(4), 721–46.

Gift, K. & Gift, T. (2015). Does Politics Influence Hiring? Evidence from a Randomized Experiment. *Political Behavior*, 37(3), 653–75.

Gilbert, G. M. (1951). Stereotype Persistence and Change among College Students. *Journal of Abnormal and Social Psychology*, 46(2), 245–54.

Goggin, S. N. & Theodoridis, A. G. (2017). Disputed Ownership: Parties, Issues, and Traits in the Minds of Voters. *Political Behavior*, 39(3), 675–702.

Goren, P. (2013). *On Voter Competence*. New York: Oxford University Press.

Graham, J., Nosek, B. A., & Haidt, J. (2012). The Moral Stereotypes of Liberals and Conservatives: Exaggeration of Differences across the Political Spectrum. *PLoS ONE*, 7, e50092.

Green, D., Palmquist, B., & Schickler, E. (2002). *Partisan Hearts and Minds*. New Haven, CT: Yale University Press.

Green, J. C. & Herrnson, P. S. (eds.). (2003). *Responsible Partisanship? The Evolution of American Political Parties Since 1950*. Lawrence, KS: University Press of Kansas.

Greene, S. (1999). Understanding Party Identification: A Social Identity Approach. *Political Psychology*, 20(2), 393–403.

Greene, S. (2004). Social Identity Theory and Party Identification. *Social Science Quarterly*, 85(1), 136–53.

Grimmer, J. & Stewart, B. M. (2013). Text as Data: The Promise and Pitfalls of Automatic Content Analysis Methods for Political Texts. *Political Analysis*, 21(3), 267–97.

Grossmann, M. & Hopkins, D. A. (2016). *Asymmetric Politics: Ideological Republicans and Group Interest Democrats*. New York: Oxford University Press.

Hamilton, D. L. & Sherman, S. J. (1996). Perceiving Persons and Groups. *Psychological Review*, 103(2), 336–55.

Harbridge, L., Malhotra, N., & Harrison, B. F. (2014). Public Preferences for Bipartisanship in the Policymaking Process. *Legislative Studies Quarterly*, 39(3), 327–55.

Harris, C. R., Coburn, N., Rohrer, D., & Pashler, H. (2013). Two Failures to Replicate High-Performance-Goal Priming Effects. *PLoS ONE*, 8, e72467.

Haslam, N., Rothschild, L., & Ernst, D. (2000). Essentialist Beliefs about Social Categories. *British Journal of Social Psychology*, 39(1), 113–27.

Hayes, D. (2005). Candidate Qualities through a Partisan Lens: A Theory of Trait Ownership. *American Journal of Political Science*, 49(4), 908–23.

Hetherington, M. J. (2001). Resurgent Mass Partisanship: The Role of Elite Polarization. *American Political Science Review*, 95(3), 619–31.

Hetherington, M. J. (2009). Putting Polarization in Perspective. *British Journal of Political Science*, 39(2), 413–48.

Hetherington, M. J. & Weiler, J. D. (2009). *Authoritarianism and Polarization in American Politics*. New York: Cambridge University Press.

Hogg, M. A. (1992). *The Social Psychology of Group Cohesiveness: From Attraction to Social Identity*. New York: New York University Press.

Hogg, M. A. & Abrams, D. (1988). *Social Identifications: A Social Psychology of Intergroup Relationships and Group Processes*. New York: Routledge.

Hoskin, M. N. (2021). The Insurrection at the U.S. Capitol Showed America that White Americans should be Concerned for their Physical Safety Also. *Forbes*, January 30. www.forbes.com/sites/maiahoskin/2021/01/30/the-insurrection-at-the-us-capitol-showed-america-that-white-americans-should-be-concerned-for-their-physical-safety-also/?sh=449d5c33107c.

Howat, A. J. (2019). The Role of Value Perceptions in Intergroup Conflict and Cooperation. *Politics, Groups, and Identities*. https://doi.org/10.1080/21565503.2019.1629320.

Huber, G. A. & Malhotra, N. (2017). Political Homophily in Social Relationships: Evidence from Online Dating Behavior. *Journal of Politics*, 79(1), 269–83.

Huddy, L. & Khatib, N. (2007). American Patriotism, National Identity, and Political Involvement. *American Journal of Political Science*, 51(1), 63–77.

Huddy, L., Mason, L., & Aarøe, L. (2015). Expressive Partisanship: Campaign Involvement, Political Emotion, and Partisan Identity. *American Political Science Review*, 109(1), 1–17.

Hutchings, V. L. & Valentino, N. A. (2004). The Centrality of Race in American Politics. *Annual Review of Political Science*, 7, 383–408.

Inbar, Y. & Lammers, J. (2012). Political Diversity in Social and Personality Psychology. *Perspectives on Psychological Science*, 7(5), 496–503.

Iyengar, S. (1996). Framing Responsibility for Political Issues. *Annals of the American Academy of Political and Social Science*, 546(1), 59–70.

Iyengar, S., Lelkes, Y., Levendusky, M., Malhotra, N., & Westwood, S. J. (2019). The Origins and Consequences of Affective Polarization in the United States. *Annual Review of Political Science*, 22, 129–46.

Iyengar, S., Sood, G., & Lelkes, Y. (2012). Affect, Not Ideology: A Social Identity Perspective on Polarization. *Public Opinion Quarterly*, 76(3), 405–31.

Iyengar, S. & Westwood, S. J. (2015). Fear and Loathing Across Party Lines: New Evidence on Group Polarization. *American Journal of Political Science*, 59(3), 690–707.

Jackson L. A., Lewandowski, D. A., Ingram, J. M., & Hodge, C. N. (1997). Group Stereotypes: Content, Gender Specificity, and Affect Associated with Typical Group Members. *Journal of Social Behavior and Personality*, 12(2), 381–97.

Josefson, J. (2000). An Exploration of the Stability of Partisan Stereotypes in the United States. *Party Politics*, 6(3), 285–304.

Kang, S. K. & Bodenhausen, G. V. (2015). Multiple Identities in Social Perception and Interaction: Challenges and Opportunities. *Annual Review of Psychology*, 66, 547–74.

Katz, D. & Braly, K. (1933). Racial Stereotypes of One Hundred College Students. *Journal of Abnormal and Social Psychology*, 28(3), 280–90.

Kelly, J. (2014). "Why are Lattes Associated with Liberals?" BBC News, October 6. www.bbc.com/news/magazine–29449037.

Key, V. O. (1949). *Southern Politics in State and Nation*. Knoxville, TN: University of Tennessee Press.

Key, V. O. (1964). *Parties, Politics, and Pressure Groups*, 5th ed. New York: Crowell.

Kinder, D. R. & Kalmoe, N. P. (2017). *Neither Liberal Nor Conservative: Ideological Innocence in the American Public*. Chicago, IL: University of Chicago Press.

King, G., Keohane, R. O., & Verba, S. (1994). *Designing Social Inquiry: Scientific Inference in Qualitative Research*. Princeton, NJ: Princeton University Press.

Klar, S. (2018). When Common Identities Decrease Trust: An Experimental Study of Partisan Women. *American Journal of Political Science*, 62(3), 610–22.

Klar, S., Krupnikov, Y., & Ryan, J. B. (2018). Affective Polarization or Partisan Disdain? Untangling a Dislike for the Opposing Party from a Dislike of Partisanship. *Public Opinion Quarterly*, 82(2), 379–90.

Kreuzer, M. (2019). The Structure of Description: Evaluating Descriptive Inferences and Conceptualizations. *Perspectives on Politics*, 17(1), 122–39.

Kunda, Z. & Spencer, S. J. (2003). When Do Stereotypes Come to Mind and When Do They Color Judgment? A Goal-Based Theoretical Framework for Stereotype Activation and Application. *Psychological Bulletin*, 129(4), 522–44.

Kuziemko, I. & Washington, E. (2018). Why Did the Democrats Lose the South? Bringing New Data to an Old Debate. *American Economic Review*, 108(10), 2830–67.

Larimer, S. (2016). Why a Trump-Backing Tow Truck Driver Says He Refused Service to a Sanders Supporter. *Washington Post*, May 5. www.washington post.com/news/the-fix/wp/2016/05/05/why-a-trump-backing-tow-truck-driver-says-he-refused-service-to-a-sanders-supporter/.

Layman, G. C. & Carsey, T. M. (2002). Party Polarization and "Conflict Extension" in the American Electorate. *American Journal of Political Science*, 46(4), 786–802.

Lee, F. E. (2009). *Beyond Ideology: Politics, Principles, and Partisanship in the U.S. Senate*. Chicago, IL: University of Chicago Press.

Levay, K. E., Freese, J., & Druckman, J. N. (2016). The Demographic and Political Composition of Mechanical Turk Samples. *SAGE Open*, 6(1), 1–17.

Levendusky, M. (2009). *The Partisan Sort: How Liberals Became Democrats and Conservatives Became Republicans*. Chicago, IL: University of Chicago Press.

Levendusky, M. S. (2010). Clearer Cues, More Consistent Voters. *Political Behavior*, 32(1), 111–31.

Levendusky, M. S. (2018). Americans, Not Partisans: Can Priming American National Identity Reduce Affective Polarization? *Journal of Politics*, 80(1), 59–70.

Levendusky, M. S., Druckman, J. N., & McLain, A. (2016). How Group Discussions Create Strong Attitudes and Strong Partisans. *Research and Politics*, April–June, 1–6.

Levendusky, M. S. & Malhotra, N. (2016a). Does Media Coverage of Partisan Polarization Affect Political Attitudes? *Political Communication*, 33(2), 283–301.

Levendusky, M. S. & Malhotra, N. (2016b). (Mis)perceptions of Partisan Polarization in the American Public. *Public Opinion Quarterly*, 80(S1), 378–91.

Levy, S. R., Stroessner, S. J., & Dweck, C. S. (1998). Stereotype Formation and Endorsement: The Role of Implicit Theories. *Journal of Personality and Social Psychology*, 74(6), 1421–36.

Lippmann, W. (1922). *Public Opinion*. New York: Harcourt, Brace, and Company.

Lodge, M. & Hamill, R. (1986). A Partisan Schema for Political Information Processing. *American Political Science Review*, 80(2), 505–19.

Mackie, D. M., Hamilton, D. L., Susskind, J., & Rosselli, F. (1996). Social Psychological Foundations of Stereotype Formation. In C. N. Macrae, C. Stangor, & M. Hewstone, eds., *Stereotypes and Stereotyping*. New York: Guildford Press, pp. 41–78.

Macrae, C. N. & Bodenhausen, G. V. (2000). Social Cognition: Thinking Categorically about Others. *Annual Review of Psychology*, 51, 93–120.

Madon, S. (1997). What Do People Believe About Gay Males? A Study of Stereotype Content and Strength. *Sex Roles*, 37(9), 663–85.

Madon, S., Guyll, M., Aboufadel, K., Montiel, E., Smith, A., Palumbo, P., & Jussim, L. (2001). Ethnic and National Stereotypes: The Princeton Trilogy Revisited and Revised. *Personality and Social Psychology Bulletin*, 27(8), 996–1010.

Martherus, J. L., Martinez, A. G., Piff, P. K., & Theodoridis, A. G. (2019). Party Animals? Extreme Partisan Polarization and Dehumanization. *Political Behavior*, 43(2), 517–40.

Mason, L. (2015). "I Disrespectfully Agree": The Differential Effects of Partisan Sorting on Social and Issue Polarization. *American Journal of Political Science*, 59(1), 128–45.

Mason, L. (2016). A Cross-Cutting Calm: How Social Sorting Drives Affective Polarization. *Public Opinion Quarterly*, 80(S1), 351–77.

Mason, L. (2018). *Uncivil Agreement: How Politics Became Our Identity.* Chicago, IL: University of Chicago Press.

Mason, L. & Wronski, J. (2018). One Tribe to Bind Them All: How Our Social Group Attachments Strengthen Partisanship. *Advances in Political Psychology*, 39(S1), 257–77.

Matthews, D. R. & Prothro, J. W. (1966). The Concept of Party Image and Its Importance for the Southern Electorate. In M. K. Jennings & L. H. Zeigler, eds.,eds., *The Electoral Process*. Englewood Cliffs, NJ: Prentice-Hall, pp. 139–74.

McCarty, N. M., Poole, K. T., & Rosenthal, H. (2016). *Polarized America: The Dance of Ideology and Unequal Riches*. Cambridge, MA: The MIT Press.

McConnell, C., Margalit, Y., Malhotra, N., & Levendusky, M. (2018). The Economic Consequences of Partisanship in a Polarized Era. *American Journal of Political Science*, 62(1), 5–18.

Moskowitz, G. B. (2010). On the Control Over Stereotype Activation and Stereotype Inhibition. *Social and Personality Psychology Compass*, 4(2), 140–58.

Mullinix, K. J. (2016). Partisanship and Preference Formation: Competing Motivations, Elite Polarization, and Issue Importance. *Political Behavior*, 38(2), 383–411.

Mullinix, K. J., Leeper, T. J., Druckman, J. N., & Freese, J. (2015). The Generalizability of Survey Experiments. *Journal of Experimental Political Science*, 2(2), 109–38.

Murphy, G. L. & Medin, D. L. (1985). The Role of Theories in Conceptual Coherence. *Psychological Review*, 92(3), 289–316.

Mutz, D. C. (2002). The Consequences of Cross-Cutting Networks for Political Participation. *American Journal of Political Science*, 46(4), 838–55.

Mutz, D. C. & Rao, J. S. (2018). The Real Reason Liberals Drink Lattes. *PS: Political Science and Politics*, 51(4), 762–7.

Nelson, L. (2014). The Most Republican and Democratic Names, in Charts. Vox, November 17. www.vox.com/xpress/2014/11/17/7233961/baby-names-political-views.

Newport, F. (2018). Top Issues for Voters: Healthcare, Economy, Immigration. Gallup, November 2. https://news.gallup.com/poll/244367/top-issues-voters-healthcare-economy-immigration.aspx.

Nguyen, H.-H. D. & Ryan, A. M. (2008). Does Stereotype Threat Affect Test Performance of Minorities and Women? A Meta-Analysis of Experimental Evidence. *Journal of Applied Psychology*, 93(6), 1314–34.

Nicholson, S. P. (2012). Polarizing Cues. *American Journal of Political Science*, 56(1), 52–66.

Niemi, R. G. & Jennings, M. K. (1991). Issues and Inheritance in the Formation of Party Identification. *American Journal of Political Science*, 35(4), 970–88.

O'Kane, C. (2019). Ellen DeGeneres Explains Friendship with George W. Bush: "We're All Different . . . That's OK." CBS News, October 8. www.cbsnews.com/news/ellen-degeneres-defends-george-w-bush-friend ship-cowboys-game-tweets-monologue-2019–10-08/.

Oliver, J. E. & Wood, T. J. (2018). *Enchanted America: How Intuition and Reason Divide Our Politics*. Chicago, IL: University of Chicago Press.

Orr, L. V. & Huber, G. A. (2019). The Policy Basis of Measured Partisan Animosity in the United States. *American Journal of Political Science*, 64 (3), 569–86.

Parker, C. S. (2010). Symbolic versus Blind Patriotism: Distinction without Difference? *Political Research Quarterly*, 63(1), 97–114.

Petrocik, J. R. (1996). Issue Ownership in Presidential Elections, with a 1980 Case Study. *American Journal of Political Science*, 40(3), 825–50.

Petrocik, J. R., Benoit, W. L., & Hansen, G. J. (2003). Issue Ownership and Presidential Campaigning, 1952–2000. *Political Science Quarterly*, 118(4), 599–626.

Pew Research Center. (2019). Partisan Antipathy: More Intense, More Personal. October 10. www.people-press.org/2019/10/10/partisan-antipathy-more-intense-more-personal.

Pew Research Center. (2020). In Changing U.S. Electorate, Race and Education Remain Stark Dividing Lines. June 2. www.pewresearch.org/politics/2020/06/02/in-changing-u-s-electorate-race-and-education-remain-stark-dividing-lines/.

Pomper, G. M. & Weiner, M. D. (2002). Toward a More Responsible Two-Party Voter: The Evolving Bases of Partisanship. In J. C. Green & P. S. Herrnson, eds., *Responsible Partisanship? The Evolution of American Political Parties Since 1950*. Lawrence, KS: University Press of Kansas, pp. 181–200.

Pope, J. C. & Woon, J. (2009). Measuring Changes in American Party Reputations, 1939–2004. *Political Research Quarterly*, 62(4), 653–61.

Prior, M. (2013). Media and Political Polarization. *Annual Review of Political Science*, 16, 101–27.

Rahn, W. M. (1993). The Role of Partisan Stereotypes in Information Processing about Political Candidates. *American Journal of Political Science*, 37(2), 472–96.

Rahn, W. M. & Cramer, K. J. (1996). Activation and Application of Political Party Stereotypes: The Role of Television. *Political Communication*, 13(2), 195–212.

Reuben, E., Sapienza, P., & Zingales, L. (2014). How Stereotypes Impair Women's Careers in Science. *Proceedings of the National Academy of Sciences of the United States of America*, 111(12), 4403–8.

Roberts, M. E., Stewart, B. M., & Airoldi, E. M. (2016). A Model of Text for Experimentation in the Social Sciences. *Journal of the American Statistical Association*, 111(515), 988–1003.

Roberts, M. E., Stewart, B. M., & Tingley, D. (2017). Stm: R Package for Structural Topic Models, Version 1.2.1. www.structuraltopicmodel.com.

Roberts, M. E., Stewart, B. M., Tingley, D., Lucas, C., Leder-Luis, J., Gadarian, S. K., Albertson, B., & Rand, D. G. (2014). Structural Topic Models for Open-Ended Survey Responses. *American Journal of Political Science*, 58(4), 1064–82.

Robison, J. (2020). Does Social Disagreement Attenuate Partisan Motivated Reasoning? A Test Case Concerning Economic Evaluations. *British Journal of Political Science*, 50(4), 1245–61.

Robison, J. & Moskowitz, R. L. (2019). The Group Basis of Affective Polarization. *Journal of Politics*, 81(3), 1075–9.

Robison, J. & Mullinix, K. J. (2016). Elite Polarization and Public Opinion: How Polarization Is Communicated and Its Effects. *Political Communication*, 33(2), 261–82.

Rogers, K. (2017). Roommates Wanted. Trump Supporters Need Not Apply. *The New York Times*, February 10. www.nytimes.com/2017/02/10/us/polit ics/roommates-trump-supporters.html.

Rogowski, J. C. & Sutherland, J. L. (2016). How Ideology Fuels Affective Polarization. *Political Behavior*, 38(2), 485–508.

Roose, K. (2020). Shocked by Trump's Loss, QAnon Struggles to Keep the Faith. *The New York Times*, November 10. www.nytimes.com/2020/11/10/technology/qanon-election-trump.html.

Rothschild, J. E., Howat, A. J., Shafranek, R. M., & Busby, E. C. (2019). Pigeonholing Partisans: Stereotypes of Party Supporters and Partisan Polarization. *Political Behavior*, 41(2), 423–43.

Rudman, L. A. & Glick, P. (2001). Prescriptive Gender Stereotypes and Backlash Toward Agentic Women. *Journal of Social Issues*, 57(4), 743–62.

Sanders, A. (1988). The Meaning of Party Images. *Political Research Quarterly*, 41(3), 583–99.

Sassenberg, K. & Moskowitz, G. B. (2005). Don't Stereotype, Think Different! Overcoming Automatic Stereotype Activation by Mindset Priming. *Journal of Experimental Social Psychology*, 41(5), 506–14.

Schaeffer, K. (2020). Far More Americans See "Very Strong" Partisan Conflicts Now than in the Last Two Presidential Election Years. Pew Research Center, 4 March. www.pewresearch.org/fact-tank/2020/03/04/far-more-americans-see-very-strong-partisan-conflicts-now-than-in-the-last-two-presidential-election-years/.

Schattschneider, E. E. (1942). *Party Government*. New York: Rinehart & Company.

Scherer, A. M., Windschitl, P. D., & Graham, J. (2015). An Ideological House of Mirrors Political Stereotypes as Exaggerations of Motivated Social Cognition Differences. *Social Psychological and Personality Science*, 6(2), 201–9.

Schildkraut, D. J. (2014). Boundaries of American Identity: Evolving Understandings of "Us". *Annual Review of Political Science*, 17, 441–60.

Schlozman, D. & Rosenfeld, S. (2019). The Hollow Parties. In F. E. Lee & N. McCarty, eds., *Can America Govern Itself?* New York: Cambridge University Press, pp. 120–51.

Sellers, C. (1965). The Equilibrium Cycle in Two-Party Politics. *Public Opinion Quarterly*, 29(1), 16–38.

Severson, A. W. (2018). Partisan Affiliation and the Evaluation of Non-Prototypical Candidates. *Journal of Experimental Political Science*, 5 (2), 121–47.

Shafranek, R. M. (2021). Political Considerations in Nonpolitical Decisions: A Conjoint Analysis of Roommate Choice. *Political Behavior*, 43(1), 271–300.

Shafranek, R. M. (2020). Political Consequences of Partisan Prejudice. *Political Psychology*, 41(1), 35–51.

Sherman, J. W. (1996). Development and Mental Representation of Stereotypes. *Journal of Personality and Social Psychology*, 70(6), 1126–41.

Sherman, J. W., Kruschke, J. K., Sherman, S. J., Percy, E. J., Petrocelli, J. V., & Conrey, F. R. (2009). Attentional Processes in Stereotype Formation: A Common Model for Category Accentuation and Illusory Correlation. *Journal of Personality and Social Psychology*, 96(2), 305–23.

Simonovits, G., Kézdi, G., & Kardos, P. (2018). Seeing the World Through the Other's Eye: An Online Intervention Reducing Ethnic Prejudice. *American Political Science Review*, 112(1), 186–93.

Sniderman, P. M., Hagendoorn, L., & Prior, M. (2004). Predisposing Factors and Situational Triggers: Exclusionary Reactions to Immigrant Minorities. *American Political Science Review*, 98(1), 35–49.

Sniderman, P. M. & Stiglitz, E. H. (2012). *The Reputational Premium: A Theory of Party Identification and Policy Reasoning*. Princeton, NJ: Princeton University Press.

Stangor, C. & Lange, J. E. (1994). Mental Representations of Social Groups: Advances in Understanding Stereotypes and Stereotyping. In M. P. Zanna, ed., *Advances in Experimental Social Psychology Vol. 26*. San Diego, CA: Academic Press, pp. 357–416.

Stangor, C. & McMillan, D. (1992). Memory for Expectancy-Congruent and Expectancy-Incongruent Information: A Review of the Social and Social Development Literatures. *Psychological Bulletin*, 111(1), 42–61.

Steele, C. M. (2011). *Whistling Vivaldi: How Stereotypes Affect Us and What We Can Do*. New York: W. W. Norton and Company.

Swanson, A. (2015). Chart: The Most Liberal and Conservative Jobs in America. *The Washington Post*, July 3. www.washingtonpost.com/news/wonk/wp/2015/06/03/why-your-flight-attendant-is-probably-a-democrat/.

Tajfel, H. (1981). *Human Groups and Social Categories: Studies in Social Psychology*. New York: Cambridge University Press.

Tajfel, H. & Turner, J. C. (1979). An Integrative Theory of Intergroup Conflict. In W. G. Austin, ed., *The Social Psychology of Intergroup Relations*. Monterey, CA: BrookeCole, pp. 33–47.

Theiss-Morse, E. (2009). *Who Counts as an American? The Boundaries of National Identity*. New York: Cambridge University Press.

Theodoridis, A. G. (2017). Me, Myself, and (I), (D), or (R)? Partisanship and Political Cognition through the Lens of Implicit Identity. *Journal of Politics*, 79(4), 1253–67.

Tine, M. & Gotlieb, R. (2013). Gender-, Race-, and Income-Based Stereotype Threat: The Effects of Multiple Stigmatized Aspects of Identity on Math Performance and Working Memory Function. *Social Psychology of Education*, 16(3), 353–76.

Todd, A. R., Bodenhausen, G. V., Richeson, J. A., & Galinsky, A. D. (2011). Perspective Taking Combats Automatic Expressions of Racial Bias. *Journal of Personality and Social Psychology*, 100(6), 1027–42.

Todd, A. R. & Galinsky, A. D. (2014). Perspective-Taking as a Strategy for Improving Intergroup Relations: Evidence, Mechanisms, and Qualifications. *Journal of Analytical Psychology*, 8(7), 374–87.

Todd, A. R., Galinsky, A. D., & Bodenhausen, G. V. (2012). Perspective Taking Undermines Stereotype Maintenance Processes: Evidence from Social Memory, Behavior Explanation, and Information Solicitation. *Social Cognition*, 30(1), 94–108.

Trilling, R. J. (1976). *Party Image and Electoral Behavior*. New York: Wiley.

Verdant Labs. (2015). Democratic vs. Republican Occupations. http://verdantlabs.com/politics_of_professions/.

Webster, S. & Abramowitz, A. I. (2017). The Ideological Foundations of Affective Polarization in the U.S. Electorate. *American Politics Research*, 45(4), 621–47.

Weingarten, E., Chen, Q., McAdams, M., Yi, J., Helper, J., & Albarracin, D. (2016). From Primed Concepts to Action: A Meta-Analysis of the Behavioral Effects of Incidentally Presented Words. *Psychological Bulletin*, 142(5), 472–97.

Weisberg, H. F. (2002). The Party in the Electorate as a Basis for More Responsible Parties. In J. C. Green, & P. S. Herrnson, eds., *Responsible Partisanship? The Evolution of American Political Parties Since 1950*. Lawrence, KS: University Press of Kansas.

Wetherell, G. A., Brandt, M. J., & Reyna, C. (2013). Discrimination Across the Ideological Divide: The Role of Value Violations and Abstract Values in Discrimination by Liberals and Conservatives. *Social Psychological and Personality Science*, 4(6), 658–67.

Wilson, C. (2016). Do You Eat Like a Republican or a Democrat? *Time*, July 18. https://time.com/4400706/republican-democrat-foods/.

Winter, N. J. G. (2010). Masculine Republicans and Feminine Democrats: Gender and Americans' Explicit and Implicit Images of the Political Parties. *Political Behavior*, 32(4), 587–618.

Wong, C. (2010). *Boundaries of Obligation in American Politics: Geographic, National, and Racial Communities*. New York: Cambridge University Press.

Yzerbyt, V., Rocher, S., & Schadron, G. (1997). Stereotypes as Explanations: A Subjective Essentialistic View of Group Perception. In R. Spears, P. J. P. J. Oakes, N.N. Ellemeres, & S. A. Haslam, eds., *The Social Psychology of Stereotyping and Group Life*. Cambridge: Blackwell, pp. 20–50.

Zaller, J. R. (1992). *The Nature and Origins of Mass Opinion*. New York: Cambridge University Press.

Acknowledgments

Numerous people helped to improve this Element throughout the research and writing process. First and foremost, we are grateful to Jamie Druckman for invaluable advice and support from the moment the project began. We also thank Doug Ahler, Jeremy Freese, Nathan Kalmoe, Alex Theodoridis, participants in the Druckman political science research lab, participants in the Thursday group at Brigham Young University, and discussants at MPSA, WPSA, and the Chicago Area Behavior Workshop for many helpful suggestions. Brandon Stewart and Matthew Lacombe provided crucial methodological advice. The series editor, Frances Lee, and two anonymous reviewers gave many helpful suggestions in the Element's final stages. All errors are our own. Finally, we thank the Political Science Department at Northwestern University, as well as Time-Sharing Experiments for the Social Sciences, for financial and material support.

Cambridge Elements ☰

American Politics

Frances E. Lee
Princeton University
Frances E. Lee is Professor of Politics at the Woodrow Wilson School of Princeton University. She is author of *Insecure Majorities: Congress and the Perpetual Campaign* (2016), *Beyond Ideology: Politics, Principles and Partisanship in the U.S. Senate* (2009), and coauthor of *Sizing Up the Senate: The Unequal Consequences of Equal Representation* (1999).

About the Series
The Cambridge Elements Series in *American Politics* publishes authoritative contributions on American politics. Emphasizing works that address big, topical questions within the American political landscape, the series is open to all branches of the subfield and actively welcomes works that bridge subject domains. It publishes both original new research on topics likely to be of interest to a broad audience and state-of-the-art synthesis and reconsideration pieces that address salient questions and incorporate new data and cases to inform arguments.

Cambridge Elements ☰

American Politics

Elements in the Series

Lightning Source UK Ltd.
Milton Keynes UK
UKHW020758121221
395354UK00016B/344